How to Make Your First Million Dollars With Airbnb

A Beginner Guide To Make Huge Cash With Airbnb

FREE BOOK REAL ESTATE MARKETING

https://ebraveboy_3ee2.gr8.com

Introduction

Rents are undoubtedly on the rise in many of the world's trendiest cities, and more so in America. It's thus becoming increasingly popular for people looking to earn some extra side money to invest in the short-term rental market. A good product that has time and again proven to be lucrative in this regard is Airbnb.

It's easy- all you need is a bit of extra living space, and you're all good, right?

Well, not exactly for the avid investor.

Unfortunately, this book is not for the regular resident of a city who wants to make some extra income off their bedroom. My target is someone a bit more ambitious, ravenous for a bigger stake, and ready for overwhelmingly robust results by investing in this fairly modest product.

In other words, I'm talking millions.

But don't get me wrong; you don't have to be an owner of properties scattered all over the place because, like most investments, and as you'll shortly see, you can begin from anywhere - even without owning any piece of property.

If you've done some research into Airbnb, you might already know that such kind of rentals currently has a higher potential for profits than the traditional long-term rentals. Airbnb rentals are rented out on a nightly basis, and the price per night is way higher than that of the standard long term rentals.

How to Make Your First Million Dollars With Airbnb

And yes, you can take into consideration factors like occupancy rate, vacancy costs, and so forth but guaranteed, it won't change the fact that an Airbnb investment would still make more profit.

I am pretty sure you've considered this kind of investment but somehow needed some important facts or deeper information to motivate you to get started, or some assurance - maybe this kind of business appears intimidating?

First of all, you're in the right place, and congratulations on making the first step to making your first million (and more millions, hopefully) with Airbnb. This book contains all the steps you need to make a successful Airbnb investment in the fastest, most effective, and sustainable way possible.

Thanks for purchasing the book. You won't regret it!

How to Make Your First Million Dollars With Airbnb

Table of Contents

Introduction ii

Airbnb: A Comprehensive Background For Beginners 6
    What Is Airbnb And How Does It Work? 6
    How Airbnb Started 7

Research 11
    Choose A Good Location 11
    Scale Up Your Research To Target A Nice City 11
    Airbnb Regulations 13
    Airbnb Market Analysis 21

Invest In Top-Class Photography 38

Airbnb Arbitrage (Strategy #2) 42
    Bonus Arbitrage Strategy: The Campus Strategy 52

Listing Your Property On Airbnb 54
    Pricing 57
    The pictures 62

How To Price Your Unit 67

Market Your Property 86

Being An Airbnb Property Manager (Strategy #3) 91

Outsourcing 107

Bonus Strategy: Try Before Buying 118

How to Make Your First Million Dollars With Airbnb

Tackling 2 Of The Most Common Issues In Airbnb Investing 122

   Buying Or Investing In Property Close To You 122

   The Potential Damages, Concerns, And Insurance 125

Conclusion 132

For the sake of those who are completely new to this, let me make a brief introduction.

Airbnb: A Comprehensive Background For Beginners

What Is Airbnb And How Does It Work?

Airbnb is an online platform where you can list or rent properties such as a sofa, spare room or an entire home for short term use- usually for travelers who don't want to stay in hotels.

As an investor, you get to use the platform to promote your space and earn some profit when customers rent your space.

Therefore, you can view this kind of a business model as one that takes a unique approach toward lodging.

When travelers browsing the site for the accommodation want to choose yours, they send an inquiry with any questions about the property or express that they want to rent it. You get the notification and host the guests if you're ready; you get your cash, and the site gets its cut (of course, it is not as simple as that, but we'll cover everything it entails in this book).

Airbnb is, therefore, a representation of a revolution in holidaying and vacationing- not just a platform. It offers a solution connecting investors and tourists, travelers or anyone looking for a place to stay temporarily.

By investing in Airbnb, you become a partner since Airbnb depends on property owners since it doesn't hold any property. Its job is to be the middleman.

Over the past couple of years, Airbnb's popularity has continued rising, leading to a shortage of inventory on the company. Most hosts report that their rates shoot up to over 90% during the peak demand months. Some of them even increase the prices of their listings, but even so, demand still stays up. This is, therefore, a huge opportunity for a prospective host like you to get a piece of their pie and create or boost your passive income.

But where did it all come from? Here's a short story of how it began.

How Airbnb Started

The story of Airbnb is very straightforward. It's a tale of how three men started renting mattresses only to end up starting a $30 billion company.

It started in 2007. Two housemates -Joe Gebbia and Brian Chesky, both of whom were designers, had a problem paying their rent on their apartment in San Francisco. They came up with the idea of selling their loft as bed and breakfast to solve their financial crisis. So they bought three air mattresses and arranged them in the loft. Two men and a woman showed up, and each one of them paid $80 to stay on a mattress.

Chesky and Gebbia realized the huge potential that the idea had and decided to get Nathan Blecharczyk, their old roommate, to help them build it into a business. They created roommates.com, a roommate-matching service, which they worked on for four months before realizing that it was a thing. They then decided to go back and work on Air, bed, and breakfast.

They launched the company for a second time, but no one noticed it.

They launched it a third time at SXSW (South by Southwest), but they only got two customers, one of whom was Chesky.

The three finished a final version of Air Bed and Breakfast before the summer of 2008 and went to pitch their idea to investors. They had redesigned the whole experience around making only three clicks to book a stay to make it easy. No one was convinced. Out of 15 investors, 8 rejected them, and seven ignored them entirely. At this point, they were bankrupt and in debt.

They decided to launch Air Bed and Breakfast once more at the Democratic National Convention in Denver in 2008. They knew there was going to be a hotel room shortage, which meant people would start looking for other options. The site, however, wasn't making anything substantial, so they opted to transform regular cereal boxes into collector's edition (products with more features than their original version) cereals boxes that they called Cap'n McCains and Obama O's. They sold these boxes on the streets for $40 each. They had attached a limited-edition number and info about their company on each one of them, and this marketing strategy worked and earned them $30, 000.

How to Make Your First Million Dollars With Airbnb

Paul Graham, the VC, noticed them and invited them to join a prestigious startup accelerator that doled out cash and training in exchange for a part of the company -known as the Y-Combinator.

The first 3 months of 2009 were spent at the accelerator, and all efforts were being made towards perfecting the product.

Nonetheless, they still got rejected during the Y combinatory by investors, but the company still carried on with its techniques in scrappy business building. While they channeled their design backgrounds, the founders launched a very ambitious project to inspire their hosts to love air, bed, and breakfast. In March 2009, the trio scrapped the 'Air, Bed and Breakfast' name and simplified it to 'Airbnb'. They then made visits to all the hosts in New Yolk to see why many properties there weren't being rented. They found out that the main issue was that the photos of the properties being listed were not of good quality. They hired a good camera and took professional pictures. This led to an instant doubling of the sales since people could see what they were paying for better.

The following month, the company received a seed investment (an arrangement where an investor invests capital in exchange for an equity stake) worth $600,000 from Sequoia Capital- and that changed a lot of things. This investment made the company hit the accelerator on growth, and the founders truly learned a lot about the business they were in. Reportedly, Chesky even lived in Airbnb for a couple of months in 2010 since their employees had crowded out the bedroom space remaining in their apartment. They were doing well.

Four years after they had their first guests (2011), the company had already become a huge name in 89 countries, and the platform had already recorded a booking of 1 million nights. The company also received an award for a breakout mobile app at SXSW, which is often described as a 'definitive success' after its lukewarm launch in 2008 at the festival.

In 2008, some of the largest VCs, in the Silicon Valley invested $112 million into the startup, and the company was valued at above $1 billion. This made Airbnb a Silicon Valley 'unicorn' (a term used to describe private startups that are valued at $1 billion or more).

The company has ever since expanded its services through many high-end launches and acquisitions near its main service, and I can gladly confirm that becoming their partner is one of the best decisions anyone can make. The company is now worth $38 billion.

Now that you have an idea of how the company started, let's go straight to the steps you should take to invest in Airbnb successfully.

At this point, I assume that you don't own any property at all. The first step is:

Research

Choose A Good Location

Just like the traditional real estate investing, location is important when it comes to Airbnb. People are always traveling and looking for a worthwhile experience; they always want to be entertained. Therefore, you have to try as much as possible to select a location that matches the experiences any potential guest would be looking for.

People are always on the lookout for various kinds of experiences- maybe they want to experience a lot of nightlife and eating out... or maybe they want a tranquil getaway in the countryside, or perhaps they're looking for a clean, cheap place to spend the night while pursuing some business ventures.

Scale Up Your Research To Target A Nice City

Since you want to make the most of your investment, you have to think wide and consider the best cities for Airbnb investing. This is simple. Just look for cities that are popular travel destinations enjoyed by business travelers or tourists within your country. An ideal city for real estate investing should have a robust economy, good transportation, shopping centers- basically as many of the essential amenities as possible.

While choosing a city, you also have to consider the most recent Airbnb trends in that city. Notably, some cities receive tourists only in certain seasons. This means that you'll have to deal with vacancies during the off-seasons.

Would you afford those vacancies? You also want to look into the economics of that particular city. If, for instance, the city is making steady growth in the tourism sector, it would be worth considering as there will be Airbnb growth in that particular city.

Last but not least, you'll have to look at the return on investment data for all the cities you choose to make an informed comparison and a good choice. So a good question you'd need to answer in this particular case is: Are the Airbnb setups there making money? Of course, the Airbnb statistics provided (by city) will assist you to find profitable Airbnb locations.

Here's a good source of these statistics:

https://www.mashvisor.com/explore/#!/Search

There are many locations on the internet where you can find reliable data on such statistics as well as the latest Airbnb analytics, particularly for cities in the U.S with a simple search.

With all the information we've talked about so far, your first step of Airbnb market research should be complete, and you might even have one or two profitable cities in mind. However, you'll still need to check out one more thing to ensure you're doing everything right: the regulations.

Airbnb Regulations

Airbnb's regulation is becoming an evolving area that has also become quite complex for local governments. While you might think this is an issue that only affects larger cities or tourist destinations, do consider the fact that there are more than 2,700 cities and counties in the U.S that have about 50 short-term rental listings.

Well, this issue is a divisive one for many communities, but arguments are mainly for the costs and benefits of allowing more short-term rentals. A significant number does celebrate the extra income for residents and a boom to the local economy, but others fear their neighborhoods' degradation and a reduction of affordable housing.

The responses from the local government have ranged from no regulation to a complete banning of short term rentals. Nonetheless, most communities haven't yet figured out an ideal way to approach this issue. A survey that involved 800 local government officials was conducted to look into the issue. This survey showed that only a quarter of them had established rules, 53% stated that they didn't have any rules while 16% were taking an active role in adopting new rules; 6% weren't sure.

Let's go back to our research.

The research

Before you start making serious decisions, you have to understand your regulation's context. It's easy to overlook this part, but any successful Airbnb investment requires understanding Airbnb regulation.

Start your research process by looking at getting a sense of the short-term market within your area. The following questions are what you should consider while doing this research:

- How many listings does the community have?
- Where are the listings located in particular? Where are the concentration areas?
- Where are the most bookings taking place?
- What are the sizes, types, and occupancy levels of housing being offered?

As an example, check out the image below, showing the current listings in Seattle.

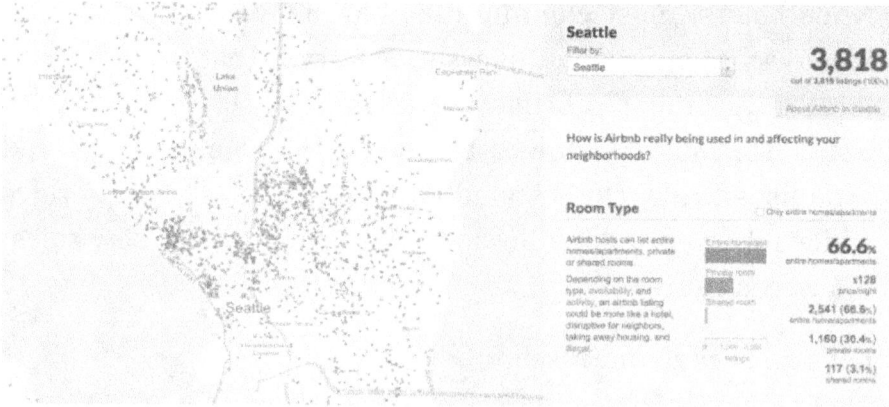

You can use insiderairbnb.com to get up-to-date data on the most recent listings in bigger cities. You can otherwise get your data directly from the site itself: Airbnb.com or any other online rental platform.

You also need to look at the local context- which relates to Airbnb regulation indirectly. The questions in this case include:

- What's the overall picture of the availability and affordability of housing in the location you select?
- How are the other existing options for lodging?
- How is the distribution of the socioeconomic demographics (class or social standing of the population) in the city?

When you get a landscape of the short-term rental market and pertinent local factors, you can begin delving into the other areas of research.

Qualitative data

Any government official will tell you that research starts getting more complicated when you begin to gather data from local stakeholders, but you can't skip this step. So, you want to be able to answer the following questions:

- Who does this issue concern in the location you are looking at?
- Who might not be in the know about what's going on, but might be affected?
- What motivates them? What do they fear?

If you're still unsure about how you can get a pulse on the residents' opinions, you can use public comment forums.

Nonetheless, you should try to frame the issue around different planning objectives. If you make short term rentals a no or yes issue, are you for them or against them? It's quite easy for stakeholders to hold opinions without putting into consideration compromise or alignment with community goals.

You should, therefore, have the discussion evolving throughout the process of regulation. The initial conversations don't have to cover each concern. You'll go back to perform a deeper stakeholder analysis after the first research phase.

Policy research

Perform due diligence on the existing Bed and Breakfast, short-term rentals, and motel laws in the chosen municipality. It's not unlikely that you'll find a few laws quite outdated, and you may be surprised at what you might find- so keep an open mind. For instance, one city had banned the serving of breakfast in Bed and Breakfasts.

You also need to take a look at the state level well. There are between 10 and 15 states that regulate short-term rentals and hotels. This is important as it determines the value of cities in which you'd like to invest i.e. in making and implementing new policies.

If the cash collected from permits and fees is going back to the state, it might not be worth the investment at a local level. Moreover, some states maintain that municipalities cannot regulate short-term rentals based on certain criteria- for instance, the length of stay, and a good number of states are changing laws very fast; it's important to keep yourself updated.

Last but not least, you also have to look beyond your local neighbors and state. How are the other communities of that size (or any other important factor) around the country and the world addressing the Airbnb regulation issue effectively?

Enforcement capacity

As you may know already, your policies will generally be shaped by what you can be able to enforce. Taking this into account early in the process- before starting to propose things publicly that you cannot enforce- is important. To guide you, consider the following questions:

- What kind of regulations can I be able to enforce with my current resources?
- What am I willing to spend on any new resources?
- What kind of regulatory environment do I want to impose on this community?
- What's the input from the individuals responsible for enforcing new laws?

Would the police department be willing to enforce a policy on prohibiting excessive noise after a particular hour? Are you considering that you may need every unit to be inspected with just one part-time inspector?

Notably, access to data can also limit some kinds of regulations. For instance, in San Francisco, it is not lawful to rent Short-term rental units for more than 90 days per year if you, the host is physically absent for that period. This kind of policy is particularly difficult to enforce without enough and reliable access to the booking data.

When you familiarize yourself with the regulations in the cities you're targeting, check how much you're willing to spend.

Set up your budget

The most appropriate investment property is one that you can afford comfortably without making a risk of defaulting on your mortgage payments, which may lead to a foreclosure. You, therefore, have to make a careful budget to achieve this goal. Consider all your regular income sources, the ongoing expenses as well as your savings. Set a maximum price that you can afford with your budget and adhere to it. As you go about the search process of your property, try to avoid getting tempted by properties that appear *perfect-* but are beyond your budget.

Note that the property's actual price isn't the only cost that will need to be covered. There are many more hidden expenses associated with purchasing an investment property like the appraisal, closing fees, property tax, inspection, insurance, and so forth. All these can total up to a lot of money.

So, set your budget and break down all the potential costs (depending on the type and location of your property) carefully. You have to include expenses like cleaning fees, repairs, landscaping, and other unexpected costs. Remember that Airbnb will take a 3% fee for each reservation.

Here's another list of the monthly costs you might need to think about:

- Property tax
- Mortgage payment
- Maintenance fee
- Insurance
- Vacancy provision
- Property management fee

Once you know how much you want to spend, you can then proceed to the next step:

Determine the most appropriate type of property

This goes without saying: the nature of your market will determine the most appropriate type of property to invest in. For instance, if you decide to go to the city center that is very busy and filled with business travelers, it would make more sense to purchase a condo or a small apartment. If you, however, decide to purchase a property in the mountains or on the beach to host friends or families on vacation, it would be smart to get a single-family home.

How to Make Your First Million Dollars With Airbnb

The type of property you choose to go with will determine the attractiveness of your property to guests, which will increase or lower your occupancy rent (and, consequently, your rental income). What's more, the rental property type you purchase also determines the price that you have to pay for it, which generally affects your return on investment.

It is, therefore, important to also think about the kind of guests you want to attract or cater to as you think about the type of property you want to acquire. To add emphasis to what I mentioned before, I have to mention that it is advisable to invest in apartments or properties that are close to city centers and tourist sites if your target group is solo tourists or travelers or couples.

Finding the property

This is one of the most daunting tasks for any real estate investor simply because they have to find a profitable property while incurring the least costs in terms of time and money. The good thing, however, is that there are many ways of finding properties that involve traditional methods like driving around the selected areas and checking properties out.

However, technology has enabled us to go about this process easily. So, the first thing you want to do before driving around is exhaust all possible sources like online listing websites (such as Mashvisor and Airdna), the real estate sections of newspapers, and information from your friends and acquaintances. After that, start looking for foreclosures, off markets, and bank-owned properties since they're often low-priced, which may push your return on investment up. As you search for your property, don't forget your budget. Keep in mind the figures you came up with to avoid falling for a property that you cannot afford.

The online listing websites typically have property tools that allow you to find and examine properties online, which makes it very easy to find good properties. The tools often use certain filters, which provide you, the user, a list of properties matching the data and criteria you input.

For instance, they use varied analytics, metrics, and real estate comparables to come up with lists of real estate properties with the highest potential of good returns in the area of your interest. They take into account your budget and the type of property you want and the returns you want.

Airbnb Market Analysis

By the time you get to this point, you should have identified a couple of Airbnb rental properties in the location or neighborhood that you want. The next thing you should do is do a comparative market analysis to, among other things, gain a good understanding of how similar properties are faring in the local real estate market and avoid bad deals, which include purchasing overpriced properties. Airbnb market analysis is, therefore, a process of finding a rental property by looking at a couple of Airbnb rental properties in the area that are similar to the one you're looking to buy. With rental comps, you're also better able to check out rental rates before you make any serious move; it also enables you to understand the relationship between the market and the fluctuation of real estate prices.

While you can get a real estate agent to do this process for you, it's more advisable to do it yourself to learn more about the field as you go about the process. As we begin, remember that comparative market analysis is not the same as the appraised value that can only be done by a licensed appraiser.

So, how do you do it?

How to perform a comparative market analysis

The first thing you need to do to conduct a comparative market analysis is to analyze the value of the property you wish to discover (or your property if you already own one). If you still don't have an idea of the properties that you'll be working with, start a property search and be very specific in your search- since prices can vary very widely, even a few blocks away- starting with your neighborhood. If you don't get any good results, go further and search for your city or any other city that you selected.

To be able to do that, look at the size of the property in square footage, the total number of rooms it contains, the construction age, its location, the available amenities and any improvements the property has recently undergone. For instance, if the property has a swimming pool, its value will increase.

Select some real estate comparables (other properties you're using for comparison- which are similar to yours)

For the comparables that you should identify, there are two conditions: the first one is that they have to be within a 1-4 mile radius from your investment property and should have gotten sold within the last 3-5 months. It is advisable to find up to five comparables (comps) whose construction, size and age, etc. is not that far from yours.

So, select a unit like yours.

For instance, if you have a 3 bed and 1 bath, start your search with that. If you cannot find an exact match, search for anything similar. Don't be surprised if you find listings within your building! That's especially possible if you're in an urban area.

What you find will be a very accurate measure of the range of prices you can charge. But you shouldn't only look at those as they could be all listed by one owner who probably doesn't have the tiniest pulse of the market- you want more data points.

Review the results

After doing all that, you want to fill out a spreadsheet with the ten most similar listings, and order them from most similar to least similar -in the spreadsheet.

As you browse the spaces within your locale, begin with properties within your building and those close to your unit. Make a pricing grid and record your results, noting the differences in amenities and prices.

You also may have to note that owing to neighborhood amenities; some streets may be pricier than others. Other things like subways on the streets and ocean views can create a large impact, and while the differences may be little, the price impact can be huge. Ensure you make a good evaluation of your market and, as much as possible, compare apples to apples.

Get two comparables and compare

When you have all your comps and gathered all the data you need about them, choose one property whose value is more than yours- it could be due to its amenities, size or location, etc.- and go ahead and select another one whose value is less than that of your property.

Armed with a price range between the two selected properties (comps), confirm that your property's price is somewhere in between the price range. Start making a comparison between the three properties in terms of factors like location, size, amenities, age, and so forth to determine the best price of your property within the real estate market. The price you determine for your property is its actual value within the real estate market (its market value).

Review the quality of your competition

The next thing you want to do is delve into the production quality of the top similar listings. The objective here is to find out or gauge their vacancy rate, popularity, and host quality. Record anything you get after answering questions like: How nice are their pictures? How many reviews do they have? How long are the reviews? Good reviews, in particular, mean that the hosts are making an effort and time into the interaction or unit. As far as popularity goes, multiple reviews per month are also a good indicator that the listing is doing very well. Along with this, you'll also need to look at the reservations- how many are taken more than two months out? Are they always nearly fully booked, half-booked, or are the weekends the only times that get booked?

On the other hand, the kind of photos the hosts display about their properties always speaks volumes about the kind of hosts they are. Have the pictures been taken on an iPhone? Roof decks or hot tubs?

Lastly, you want to take a look at the host metrics. Ask yourself these and more questions:

- What is the host's response rate and the average response time?

- How much effort did the host put into their profile?

- How are the reviews about the host, and how does the host respond to the negative reviews? For instance, if the host doesn't often respond to negative reviews, then they are not taking the business as seriously as you would- right? It would, therefore, mean that there is an opportunity right there.

- Do the reviews contain any trends that you can capitalize on? Remember that the standard response rate is 100%.

This will bring ideas about what you should do with your space, the best ways to boost your listing as well as your position.

Any real estate expert will tell you that it's important to get acquainted with these and more tiny details for several units to understand your market fully and, among other things, know which weaknesses to take advantage of going forward.

Now that you know how to select properties based on the various factors available today, you might still wonder how your unit stacks up. It's okay and normal to have such concerns, especially when you've not completed the process as discussed up to this point.

However, let me give you an example to let you see how easy this is:

If you get a unit somewhere whose size is similar to yours but contains great professional pictures, over 50 five-star reviews, and many extra services and gifts like free surfboards or welcome wine gifts, then you won't charge as much as them- as you are just getting started. However, if there is a unit out there somewhere that looks quite worse than yours in the pictures and has very few reviews, you can leverage on that and set a higher price.

The idea is to see where your property fits in the market place and get a price from there.

The numbers

If any of this has felt a little daunting, let me assure you that purchasing a property and renting it out makes financial sense. My assumption so far is that the property you found is strategically located in a major city.

How to Make Your First Million Dollars With Airbnb

Let's see a practical example of a small existing unit in San Francisco. The numbers break-down on the apartment is as follows:

The buying price is $450K

20% down is $90K

The loan acquired for the property is $360K. This is a 7-year ARM (adjustable-rate mortgage) at 3.25% for a 30-year term

The payments total up to $2000 per month (this includes insurance interest, taxes and so forth)

HOA (Home Owners Association) dues: $500 per month

This totals to $2500 per month

This means that to break even on this particular unit; the owner has to make at least $2500 per month.

Let's take a look at a typical month:

- The total number of bookings is 7
- The total number of nights rented is 25
- This means that the average nights per booking is 3.7
- In this unit, the average cost per night is $175
- This brings the gross revenue to $4375

How about the costs?

- Cleaning total up to $350 since each booking is $50

How to Make Your First Million Dollars With Airbnb

- The supplies total up to $175. These are things like wine, tissue paper, coffee and chocolate which total up to $25 per booking

- Utilities (such as cable TV, internet and power) total up to $200

- This totals to $725

Therefore, this leads to the net: $1,150

Therefore, when this owner breaks it all down, he gets a net of more than $1,000 each month while building equity in the unit. The owner discloses that the hot months such as May, June and July net slightly more, but months like January and December net a little less. However, the average net per month is over $1,000.

Shall we continue? I'll take that as a yes.

So, when you purchase your property, you have to optimize it for Airbnb by making some renovations. It doesn't matter if you want to host multiple properties or a single room since all the properties have to draw in clients.

You have to note that just like cars, property furnishings depreciate over time, and unless you bought a new property, you might need to reinvest in new furnishings and renovations in the unit —where necessary- to increase the asset's value. Indeed, there is a correlation between a unit's listing quality and the price you can charge per night. Just remember that this is not a linear relationship.

Effect of Renovation on Price

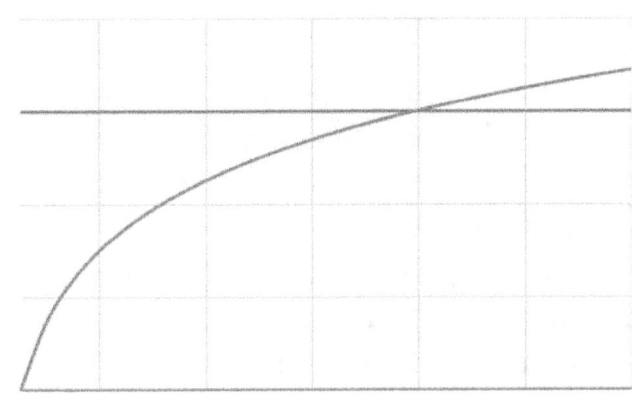

Renovation & Furnishing Spend

Therefore, you may need to keep your renovations economical and minimal if you want to maximize on the property. As you can see in the graph above, it's possible to over-renovate- but unfortunately, the higher you go, the less the price will change. It doesn't matter if your décor is the most gorgeous, as other factors like location and the basic value of the property will have a role to play.

The bottom line is, don't overdo it.

As we begin looking at some basic renovation ideas you should consider, remember that one of the best primary investments that will increase your occupancy as well as the nightly rate is increasing the number of beds. For instance, a pull-out couch would allow for two more guests, which makes it more flexible for you in terms of the number of guests your unit can accommodate.

Let's begin.

Basic renovations ideas

It's highly likely that you'll purchase an old (even if it's 1-year old) rental and decide to renovate it by using the least amount of cash possible. The good news is that you don't have to spend a lot on expensive renovations to turn your rental space into one that will lure potential guests into clicking that booking button straightaway. This section explores some of the tips of making such renovations on a budget by putting special focus on major areas in a rental that typically require it.

1. Floor

We both know that flooring plays a massive role in the overall look of any housing unit. If the property contains old linoleum or strained carpeting, it may be necessary to update your floor. Today, most guests prefer hardwood floors, but as we both know, hardwood floors can be fairly expensive to install. Nonetheless, the first thing you need to note is that some homeowners have genuine hardwood floors hidden beneath their outdated carpets.

If your newly acquired home reflects the statement above, get rid of the carpet and refinish the hardwoods. Such a project often involves lots of sanding and (then) finishing using a sealant. If you want the floors to have a particular color, you can stain them as well. It can take a lot of work to refinish hardwoods, but it's generally inexpensive, and you can be able to finish it in one weekend.

If you have to install a fresh floor, there are many inexpensive flooring options. You can always pay attention to the spaces your guests will be using and only redo the flooring in those specific rooms to spend less. You should also consider looking for wood laminate flooring or even getting something affordable yet unique such as a polished concrete floor.

Create more storage space

Though often overlooked, storage space can be a selling point of any unit. Guests always love storage space, and adding a little more storage space in a room with limited storage will create a win-win situation. Just make sure you add storage that matches the overall feel of the space. If you want a modern look, try installing chic and modest floating shelves. If you want a more classic look, you may need to create some built-ins.

Something as simple as a couple of hooks on the wall, some free closet space, or a shoe rack by the door can make a big difference for guests. Airbnb recommends having about 8-10 empty hangers for guests to hang their clothes. Don't forget that upgrading the storage in your property doesn't have to break your bank. You can finish it in one afternoon.

Paint the kitchen cabinets

Particularly, if you're planning on renting out your unit for longer stays, the kitchen area may be a determining factor for guests. In any case, one of the biggest advantages of an Airbnb over a typical hotel is that the guests can access the kitchen. It makes sense, therefore, that most of them will be paying lots of attention to your kitchen pictures. Kitchen remodels are very popular for the ROI (Return on Investment) that homeowners expect from them. Another surprising fact is that major kitchen remodels don't have as much ROI as minor kitchen remodels. You should thus consider doing a few touches in that room if it already looks fine- to perfect it. If it's outdated though, start by painting all the cabinets and replace the cabinet doors whenever necessary - if you have a coin or so to spare. You can also add crown molding to the top to bring a more sophisticated touch to the room. Read this for more information on that:

http://bit.ly/2Xhmekf

Here's a little info on that though:

The crown molding

If the unit doesn't have enough (or any) crown molding, you can install the pieces yourself by following the steps outlined in the tutorial above. It's the perfect architectural detail that's sure to make any room look more high-end and complete. Most people shy away from this kind of project because they think it's too difficult (to do it themselves) or too expensive. All you need to complete this project is a crown molding kit, and you'll be surprised how cheap and easy this simple renovation project is.

With just a few simple steps, you'll be having a very beautiful crown molding in your unit. It doesn't matter whether you've done a property renovation before, as you can take advantage of crown molding kits like these (http://bit.ly/2CEoupg), which are generally easy to use- so much that anyone can do it. Psst! Do you want to know something? It means that you don't need to worry about getting studs or even filling nail holes, among other things- cool, huh?

Add a coffee nook

You might hate coffee, but many people out there love it. It doesn't matter if your next guest will be on vacation or business, but they'll most likely spend most days outside; your rental will be their little home base at the start and end of each day they'll be around. You'd agree with me that giving them a special area to start their day or unwind at the end of the day with a warm cup of coffee is a lovely idea.

But what if your kitchen is small?

In that case, you can set aside a corner to a coffee cart or a corner shelf with a good coffee maker, a grinder, French press, and a can of fresh coffee beans. Along with this, you can also add a small table with two stools or chairs, and your lovely nook will be complete. Just ensure you accentuate this area in nice pictures, and sit back and wait for the coffee lovers to gush in.

Freshen up your walls

Fresh paint can make a huge difference in your new house. Regardless of the type or function of any unit, painting is always a perfect way to freshen up space and make everything pop for a fairly low price. If you want to keep it as affordable as you possibly can, be on the lookout for paint discount promotions from large paint brands or home development stores. If you're not sure of the color for your walls, experts always say that you can never go wrong with white. You can also have a combination of beige and gray if you want a cool neutral color. It's actually on the trend.

If you're completely new to this and want to have a rough estimate of the amount of paint that you would need, add all the widths of all the walls you want to paint and multiply the number by the height of the walls. Lastly, divide the number you get by 350- this is the square footage that each gallon of paint would typically cover. This will give you a good idea of the number of gallons of paint you require.

Make an accent wall

An accent wall is simply a wall that contains texture or color that generally stands out from the other walls in the unit. Ideally, you should choose one wall and turn it into a nice accent wall; ensure it's the one behind the guest's bed- just for a cool focal point.

Other inexpensive ways you can create a nice accent wall is as follows:

Paint- You can go with a bold color like orange, bright green, or navy. You may need to do some research, though, to see the kind of colors that are trending at the time you reach this point in your project.

Decal- Decals come in sheets or rolls, and are specifically made to peel and stick, making them very easy and quite inexpensive as means of dressing up a wall. Without a doubt, a wall decal can convert any plain wall into a work of art.

Wallpaper- Some people think wallpapers are a thing of the past, but with a little looking around, you may be surprised to find extremely chic, modern wallpapers that will make you want to redesign your own home. If your unit, however, has a more antique or rustic feel, you can select wallpaper with a little traditional design.

Wood- You can also use wood planking to create a lovely look that looks at home in any space- whether it's from a shabby-chic farmhouse or an industrial or ultramodern house. Remember to look for any inexpensive used wood (if you fail to get them for free) that you can reclaim.

Upgrade the bathroom tile

An image of a nice, modern bathroom will give potential guests an instant vision of bathing in a comfortable, relaxing space. If your bathroom wall is covered in tile from ten years ago, it almost impossible to turn it into a modern bathroom. Just replace the floral-print or pink tile with modern designs to make the space more contemporary and upscale.

Can you do it yourself?

Yes. To remove the old tiles, grab a regular utility knife and score the grout around the tiles; using a chisel and hammer, pop off the tiles one by one. After removing the old tiles, you'll have several options to choose from. For instance, you can use laminate that looks like tile, purchase new tiles to replace the old ones or sand the walls and paint them. Whatever you choose, it's highly likely it'll make a huge improvement on those outdated tiles.

Update the décor

If making more serious renovation around the unit appears daunting, remember that you can make your unit look great simply by updating its décor. Just select a theme or a particular style and stick to it. It doesn't matter whether you want to go traditional, minimalist, or use it to express your bohemian nature; you can add a couple of important pieces to the room and make it more inviting and looking more polished.

Some great additions can be anything from new curtains, new wall hangings, a new set of beddings, or a nice accent piece. The point of having a new décor is to make the room feel "put-together" and clean.

Whatever décor you add, remember to avoid cluttering up space so that the guests have a lot of space to set their stuff. When a prospective guest sees a room that is beautifully decorated in your area, he/she may be more drawn to it than the others.

Add some nice lighting

There's nothing that brightens up the feel of a house like lighting. If the house feels dark, find strategic places to add some lamps or light fixtures in the ceiling or wall. Definitely, the unit you acquired does have existing light fixtures, but you should consider whether they're boosting or hurting your room's appearance. While they may appear to be neutral, you can consider bringing a touch of uniqueness and interest in the plainest of rooms by replacing them.

How to Make Your First Million Dollars With Airbnb

Pay close attention to the kitchen and dining area lighting. Upscale and ultramodern light fixtures can appear stunning, but they can also be costly in some cases. You can save by skipping the middleman and purchasing directly from the manufacturer. You can also look for antique lighting fixtures in your resident flea market and creatively upcycle them to have unique pieces. A nice way of sprucing up existing light fixtures is by fixing a ceiling medallion around them. Such molded medallions usually come in different designs, most of which add a touch of elegance to any space.

Your listing looks pretty fancy now- peppered with top-end amenities and all... it's also probably in a great location and seemingly ready to make money for you! But not so fast! Before you think of listing the property on Airbnb, do the following:

Invest In Top-Class Photography

Pictures are everything. Listings that have better photos get booked a lot more often.

You, therefore, need to consider taking time when planning this part out. You also need to note that pictures help with the Click-through rate on the search page. A poor picture means people will be scrolling past you.

You can start by choosing a photographer privately or with Airbnb, and from there, follow the tips below to assist you to sail through perfectly while getting the most of your pictures.

Consider the target audience

When taking photos, you need to consider who you're renting to. This includes groups like business people, families who have young kids, and couples. Each one of such groups will be looking for different things in the picture.

For instance, if you're targeting business people, you have to consider that they will be looking to see nice desks, printers, Wi-Fi, additional monitor with cables, means of making quick meals and coffee/tea and comfortable beds to relax after work. Families, on the other hand, want to see a lot of space to unpack and store their luggage, a nice kitchen for meals and so on. Couples want to see great couches to lounge on, dining area, and a comfortable bed.

You, therefore, have to look at the functional needs of the specific group(s) of people you are targeting.

Secondly, you want to optimize your photography to reflect the emotional needs of your guests. I can describe this as what you hear as 'a sense of [_____]". For instance, a sense of luxury.

Take a look at the examples below that are used to describe emotional benefits some types of guests look forward to experiencing, and you can inspire such feelings in the images of your listings.

- Families have a sense of security: the gates should be highlighted, CCTV cameras, perhaps an image of kids playing outside the unit, and anything else you can think of.

- Couples want to feel luxurious: you can, therefore, add complimentary champagne and flutes on the table, large pillows, and a nice bed.

- Business people often want to feel rewarded: you can highlight premium amenities and a premium view.

- Tourist groups want a sense of excitement: highlight nightlife shots, big congregation places, view of the hills, etc.

Other things to consider when taking images

Your positioning

You'll most likely have a TV; so what brand is it? Is it a tube or a flat-screen? Either type will depict and promote varying ideas about your place. Nice flat screens generally bring a premium halo effect to your unit. A hallo effect is simply a situation where the first impression can answer any subconscious question or make assumptions. You have to promote stuff in your unit that will create a positive halo effect.

Your built-in equities

I am talking about parts of your unit —inside and outside- you can accentuate what's not offered anywhere else. For instance, you may have mountainside scenery, beautiful exotic gardens, a unique lake view, a nice indoor personalized Jacuzzi, and so forth. You need to show these off and attract more prospective guests.

How your rental looks like

This is where you avoid negative reviews.

How will your property look like each time a guest walks through the door? You need to be honest. If you're not offering some things, or you are planning on removing some items from the pictures- perhaps 'to be safe', then avoid showing them. Most people will remember, visually, what they see on the site and will want the same replicated on the ground. As you know, lying is one of the quickest ways to annoy guests (especially if you raised their hopes that you have certain amazing products, and that you've got some integrity to represent your place accurately) and get bad reviews.

Your property doesn't have to be the best on the block; all you need to do is be truthful about what you're offering.

How to Make Your First Million Dollars With Airbnb

Simplicity

You know that pictures can be worth many words, but nobody has time for that. Avoid jam-packing your images with too many amenities. You can just take multiple shot angles of a large room or emphasize parts of your entertainment area (for instance), not all the components you own!

At this point, you can go ahead and list your property on Airbnb and move on to the next marketing strategies. But before we delve into that, let's make another supposition:

What if you want to include a space owned by another person, perhaps a typical rental house (that you could be living in) that you think would do well with Airbnb?

Airbnb Arbitrage (Strategy #2)

Fewer people today can purchase homes in the current economy. Across the United States, home prices are sharply increasing, and the median wages aren't meeting the necessary level to be able to buy homes.

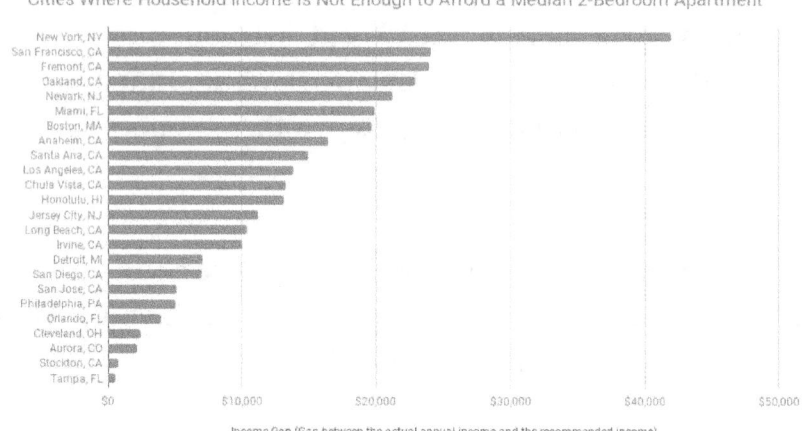

This, therefore, excludes many people from participating in the short-term rental business if the traditional vacation rental path is taken. This, however, means that potential entrepreneurs like you have an opportunity in the field of rental arbitrage (where you use someone's product- or property in this case- and sell it elsewhere).

With all we've discussed so far, though, it may seem easy to go this route because anyway, you get to skip many steps we covered earlier typical to owning your property and using it for Airbnb. However, this one has its unique challenges, but the biggest one so far is getting the owner of the property to get on board. How do you approach the owner of the property and convince them to allow you to use their property for this kind of investment?

A rental, even one that you may be living in right now, can widen your Airbnb investment portfolio; the fact that it comes with very little upfront costs makes it very attractive and ideal to use. But I'm sure you already know that, so let's talk about the biggest issue with this one: the big conversation.

"But what's the big deal?" You may be tempted to think.

"Why would my landlord or any landlord care?"

This is a very common first reaction and a prime reason why many people rent on Airbnb without informing the owners of the properties involved. But that's not a good idea. Well, doing so may work for a short while, but it's almost always going to blow up in your face - eventually. Therefore, you stand to lose more than your rental money; you could get evicted. Additionally, you don't want to lower your odds of getting permission by trying to approach the conversation after getting caught.

Get into the owner's mind

First of all, you need to understand the position the owner is coming from to stand a chance of negotiating with them. Understand how they view Airbnb clearly. Put yourself in their shoes and try thinking about the things that influence their decisions and how they view their properties.

Here's a little information you need to have first:

While some owners make lots of cash off their properties and others relatively low income (side income), one thing always remains constant: all these owners always view long-term rental income as a low-risk investment.

Imagine if you were the owner; you put lots of effort in making renovations and ensuring you signed in tenants, and then made efforts to help the tenants enjoy their stay. You know very well that in as much as you'd want to make the most of your property, it would still generate you the same amount of cash each month for your tenants' lease terms. This means that logically, you wouldn't see the need to invest a lot more money and energy into the property- you're seeing it as a long-term, fixed income stream. You'd consider any extra effort spent on the rental a waste of time.

The worst-case scenario for you, in this case, would be losing a tenant or your property getting damaged. But tenants can be replaced, and you can purchase insurance to cover property damage.

But you're still the owner; now imagine a tenant comes to you and requests if they can intermittently let in many strangers in and out of their space for their profit! That right there changes the property from being low risk/modest income to high risk/ modest income.

The risks

There are a couple of reasons that make a high property risk for landlords.

They include the following:

- Even though Airbnb verifies guests for the host, there always is a chance that bad-apple guests could come and damage parts of the property, disturb or harass neighbors or even steal.

- Short-term rentals are illegal in a good number of city municipalities.

- Landlords/landladies are obligated to have "homeowners" insurance for their property to cover anything that could go wrong. The problem is that this kind of insurance usually denies any claim in the instance they find out that space was being used for business purposes- and Airbnb is a good example. What's worse is that the landlord/landlady's insurance could be canceled entirely, which would make the whole building illegal.

- And don't forget that this whole risk is being taken without any potential inside. That simply doesn't make sense.

It is extremely difficult to find a landlord who is very okay with you using their property to make money without asking something in return.

So, what do you do/say?

While paying more rent is all it takes in many cases, you may need to be prepared to look at other factors concerning your relative position before you get into the conversation.

These include things like:

- How long you've been their tenant, and your record
- How fast (you think) they can find another long-term tenant- whether it is a hot rental market.
- Whether the landlord has other properties.
- Other tenants who could be affected.

Having a strong negotiating position means that (among other things):

- You've been their tenant for a long time, and the landlord is quite comfortable with you
- Your landlord understands Airbnb, and he only has a few properties

So, what can you offer your landlord?

Particularly, if you're in a weak position, you might need to consider this to get a yes. Some of the things you can offer any landlord include the following:

- Extending your lease
- Offering to pay more- perhaps a certain percentage of your Airbnb earnings
- Paying pre-pay rent upfront

As regards to the risk, you can enlighten them on Airbnb's [$1,000,000 insurance guarantee](), and have them know that it works.

You can also offer to buy your vacation rental insurance- which ranges between $80 and $200 per month. Please [read more](http://bit.ly/2NLOCrF) about it before making a move: http://bit.ly/2NLOCrF

You can also think of limiting the rentals to certain periods and maybe certain groups of people. Maybe you can guarantee that you'll only rent private rooms and will be present during the entire stay.

You can revise your rental contract to cover particular damages yourself and increase the amount of your security deposit.

Definitely, this is not an exhaustive list of all the available options, but they are a good place to start. All you need to do is be ready to know what you think you can offer them and what it will take to attend to their concerns.

But before we move on to the next step, let me give you an idea of one option you may have in responding to your landlord/landlady if they're not open to Airbnb.

The last resort

If the landlord/landlady is completely not open or receptive to this idea, you can go ahead and look for their legal counsel. In 9 out of 10 cases, landlords will have some legal counsel with whom they work on things like insurance, contracts, tenant rights, and so forth.

You can either contact the lawyer and state your case or use your lawyer to talk on your behalf. Given the fact that any lawyer has a duty to represent their client's best interest, he/she will have to listen to you as you're presenting an opportunity for their client to make more money, an opportunity that is completely legal and within the local laws.

The good thing is that it is going to be very difficult for the landlord/landlady to say no when their legal counsel tells them that the opportunity is legal, and it can work.

An example

After a while of investing in Airbnb using properties he'd been buying, Dave decided to try rental arbitrage to increase his income. At first, he started experimenting by renting out his home in Austin, Texas, when he traveled. During March and April, he made $ 7, 687, when his rent and utilities would have amounted to about $3,600. His rented house is in the downtown area, and as you know, March is the SXSW month, which is the largest money earner for short-term rentals in Austin. Nonetheless, he had an interesting dilemma since April was also a very profitable month as well, which made him feel like living in his own house was costing him money.

He, therefore, approached his landlord and asked him if he would allow him to rent half of his duplex. After telling him upfront what he wanted to do, he gave the green light. The landlord also owned other places within the town and after a couple of discussions, the landlord also agreed to offer them to Dave for his Airbnb project (I imagine his (landlord's) cut must have been motivating). Eventually, Dave had listed 6 properties- a one-bedroom house and five two-bedroom houses. Dave reveals that within his first 8 months, he netted a profit of $10, 546. 10. Here's the breakdown:

How to Make Your First Million Dollars With Airbnb

	October, 2017	November, 2017	December, 2017	January, 2018	February, 2018	March, 2018	April, 2018	May, 2018	Total
Revenue	$3,546.32	$2,920.67	$3,971.44	$2,810.09	$2,296.48	$6,588.46	$3,394.75	$2,475.93	$28,004.14
Expenses	-$1,922.65	-$2,043.16	-$2,157.66	-$2,222.42	-$2,109.24	-$2,443.65	-$2,352.56	-$2,206.70	-$17,458.04
Net Total	$1,623.67	$877.51	$1,813.78	$587.67	$187.24	$4,144.81	$1,042.19	$269.23	$10,546.10

In case you're wondering, the expenses included all the monthly expenses such as cleaning, rent, and utilities.

This is Dave's experience during his initial Airbnb investing period. You can imagine how much he gets from his entire investment today. Being one of the most successful rental arbitrage investors currently, it's only courteous to mention a few key points of his advice to anyone getting into this kind of investment.

Key points to note

1. Dave notes that many people tend to set their prices based on their expenses. These people tend to either quit or raise their prices too much when they don't realize 'enough' profits. According to Dave, you need to go below the market rent. To do so, you have to be creative; for instance, you have to look for a property owner/ landlord who is not very fulfilled at managing their properties.

Other ways to set your prices will be discussed in this book.

2. You need to get the owner's approval before renting out their property while having at the back of your mind the fact that not everyone is okay with Airbnb. Dave notes that some owners have the delusional opinion that people living in their properties for a short period

can cause problems with people living there for a longer-term. To get around this problem, he emphasizes the importance of being creative in your pitch. For instance, Dave pitches to his owner using the following simple ideas:

- That he is financially motivated to maintain the property in the best shape possible to keep the property competitive and leaving good reviews on Airbnb.

- That he will be getting the property cleaned every week by professional cleaners.

- That he would have to renew the lease given the amount of money spent on furnishing and the high returns he (Dave) would be getting.

Dave also notes that besides that, particularly when he meets a nervous landlord, he makes sure to address the issue of property damage before they ask. He also makes sure they understand that with Airbnb, they'd no longer have to follow tenants around to make payments (something which all of them have to grapple with) since Airbnb payment is done when the guest books which means that he (Dave) will send the payment to the landlord during the check-in day. Who would refuse that?

3. Dave notes that his success has also been attributed to the location of his properties as well as targeting events taking place locally. For instance, he notes that for a 6-bedroom house located in downtown Austin, they were able to charge $2,000 per night for a period of one year

for SXSW. All the other places that could accommodate all the groups that large were often sold out, and the rest a bit further from downtown were charging as high as over $3,000 per night since there were very few places left. It wasn't difficult to get his place booked.

4. If you want to try rental arbitrage, he advises that you should ALWAYS get a property in good condition. Ideally, if not new, you can get a property that requires minor renovations or upgrading for purposes of improving it- not one that would require a total overhaul. To him, old properties always gave him a nightmare. Based on his experience, he notes four major reasons why you should never rent an old house regardless of the price tag.

- You'll experience too many complaints, cancellations, and refunds since there always will be problems with the property (unless you change and upgrade everything, which will not make any financial sense).

- You'll get bad reviews, which will negatively affect your rank in the search algorithm. You want a perfect ranking, which you'll never get if your property keeps weighing your efforts down. Also, your account ranking will be affected, which means that all the other properties might get hurt in the process.

- If you're looking to automate your business, it will be a problem because there will be issues every day about broken things and complaints all the time.

- Remember that your relationship with your landlord will also be affected negatively as well since stuff in old properties always break or break down. Imagine having to fix the roof, AC, the plumbing, and so forth now and then since your landlord is not as motivated as you to fix such things quickly as you. Resorting to fix these things by yourself might hurt your financial health.

Bonus Arbitrage Strategy: The Campus Strategy

Take this scenario as an example:

You have a 6 bedroom house that you're paying for $3,000 per month. If you think that it's way too cheap to be real, go and ask around large campuses. Large houses on campus typically have huge discounts on rent because they're intended for large groups of students, and as you may know, students are pre-leases.

When a large house is pre-leased for next year when the current school year has already begun, the landlords are always desperate to fill it. Who else do you think would want to rent a 6-bedroom house for just 9 months?

If you're still not convinced, here are the monthly results of one investor who uses this strategy to get some side cash off Airbnb:

How to Make Your First Million Dollars With Airbnb

	November, 2017	December, 2017	January, 2018	February, 2018	March, 2018	April, 2018	May, 2018	June, 2018	July, 2018	
Revenue		3533.71	4417.38	5703.6	14302.36	5903.42	6975.62	4782.1	4063.33	49,681.52
Expenses	-1275.47	-3562.62	-4445.01	-3863.53	-4175.2	-4070.79	-4091.17	-4150.09	-4126.43	-33,760.31
Net Total	-1275.47	-28.91	-27.63	1840.07	10127.16	1832.63	2884.45	632.01	-63.1	15,921.21

As you can see, the guy netted $15, 921 before the deposit. It may not seem very profitable (and I wouldn't advise you to go all out with it), it is a great strategy if you have a plan for what to do with the furniture you acquire after the lease expires. For instance, if you plan on purchasing a house the following year, or have a huge garage to store stuff as you continue looking for another deal during summer, it could work for you. All you need to make sure you understand are the costs and revenue estimates of your area. Remember that this is just another idea for a deal; if you can be able to get a longer-term deal to keep you from moving every year, that's better.

Before we talk about the third strategy of making money off Airbnb, let's break the flow by looking at how you can list, price and market your property- just in case you're starting to get bored.

How to Make Your First Million Dollars With Airbnb

Listing Your Property On Airbnb

First, go to Airbnb.com and choose the option "list your space" in the homepage's top right corner. You'll be redirected to a form that will prompt you to fill in the general details of your place. Note that you can finish this first form before you create your account. Therefore, you may want to sign up before you start.

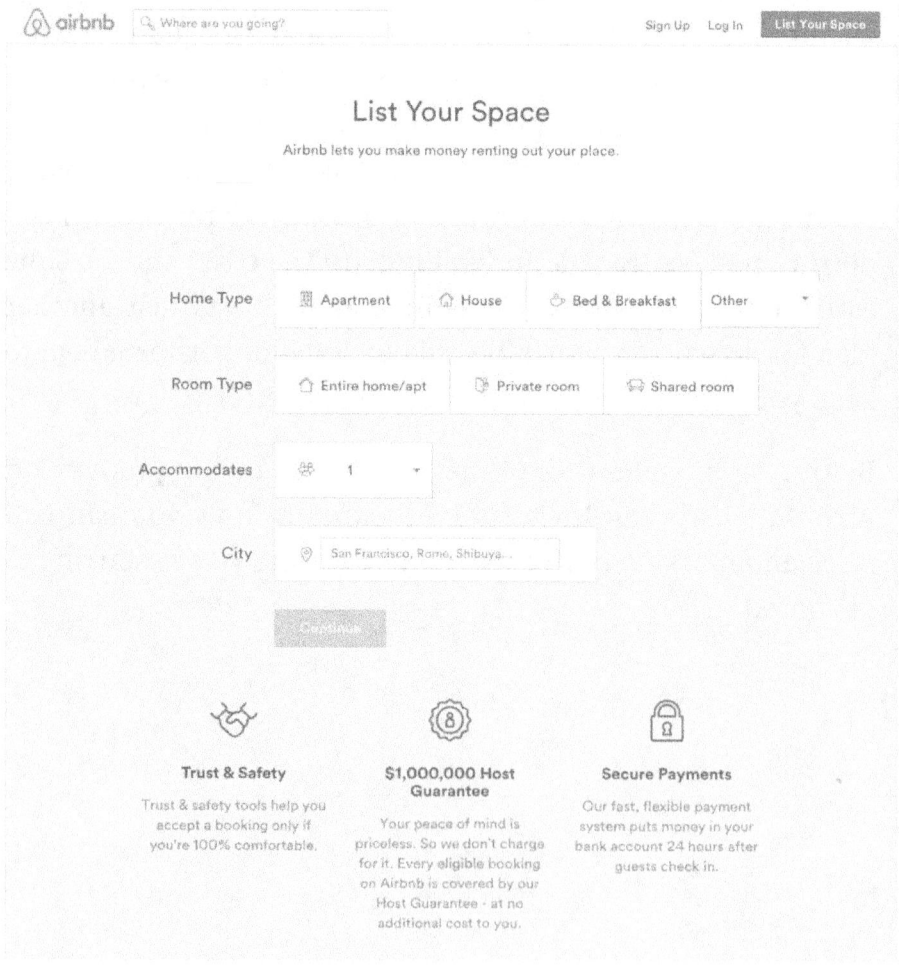

- The "home type": The options here are very straightforward. There is a small description of each home type that appears when the mouse hovers over. All you need to do is select an option that best describes your property. Remember that the drop-down menu to the right side significantly expands the list of your choices, and this includes everything from tents, lofts to castles, and so forth.

- The "room type": This part is one of the most important since your guests as well as you may be particular about having a certain degree of privacy. Therefore, ensure you build your listing accurately enough to attract the most suitable guests for your property. Just like the previous option, Airbnb offers brief definitions of their terminology here to assist you in selecting the option that best describes your property.

  Nonetheless, you need to note that before you select "entire home/apartment," you need to keep it in mind that giving your guests exclusive access to the entire property might include access to other amenities on the property (assuming you're renting out part of your own home), which may include things like the pool or garage. On the other hand, a "private room" includes more home-sharing than you might expect, like that of any connecting rooms, kitchens, and bathrooms. Additionally, you may not be able to change the number of beds offered in this listing unless you choose "entire home/ apartment." All the other options will register your property with one bed automatically.

- "Accommodates." This part lets you choose the maximum number of people you can have in your listing comfortably. For now, you can calculate the number of people you can accommodate if everyone had their bed, inflatable mattress or sofa bed- as long as the sleeping arrangement is as comfortable enough. Put yourself in the shoes of your prospective guests to see whether you'd be comfortable. Lastly, choose the right number of guests from the drop-down list provided.

- "City": Type in the name where the property you're listing is located while choosing to continue to move on to the following step.

At this point, you will have to fill in more specific details about your listing. This part is split into sections, which makes it very simple to cover all the information if you take it from the top and fill out the sections in the order that they appear on the list. Note that if a booking is secured with an inaccurate listing, you won't be able to change the listing's defective criteria without sending a modification request to the guest in question. This, in particular, could cost you one booking and time. Therefore, try to be as diligent with your details as possible, since a little error can have a huge impact.

Also, don't forget that you can return and edit the descriptions provided. You can also utilize the 'preview' button in your screen's top corner to see how your potential guests will be seeing your content.

The calendar

How to Make Your First Million Dollars With Airbnb

You'll also have three options to specify the availability of the property you're currently listing. These options generally reflect the period within which you want your property to remain listed with Airbnb, as opposed to specifying the actual rental dates. You can go with the 'always' option to have it listed indefinitely, only for certain days or 'sometimes' for fixed durations or 'one time' to have it limited to one fixed duration. You should fill in the specific dates for rental when you publish your listing and wait to be updated regularly.

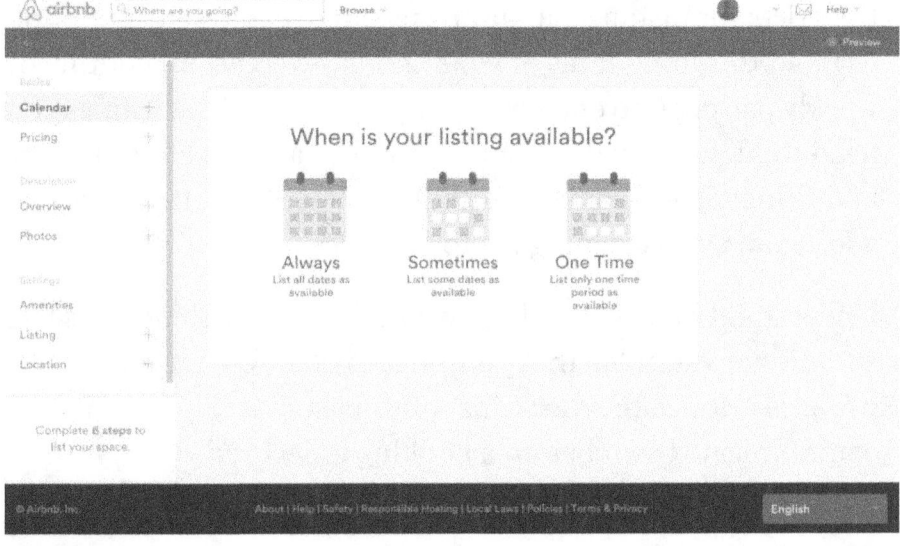

Pricing

The site will suggest the amount of money you should charge based on the details you provide as well as the trends that are shaping the local rental market currently, like increased tourism, holidays and so much more.

You'll have the option of playing around with the price generator, but if this is your first time listing a unit on the site,

Airbnb will recommend starting below the suggested rate. This will assist you to get a foot in the door before you get the opportunity to increase your profile reviews, among other credentials. You should, however, remember that it's important to stay competitive and relevant, so take this step further by going back to the step where you make comparisons of similar Airbnb listings in your area.

Besides the general listing qualities and market activity, there is another set of factors you have to consider when calculating the price; for instance, it may be useful to exercise your option to mold the going rates of your listing by creating monthly or weekly packages to encourage longer rentals. Other things you need to factor ahead of time in are the taxes, cost of utilities, and things like cleaning. With Airbnb, you get the option of adding an extra cleaning fee to the price.

Understand that even though you cannot include these in situational variables that you plan to charge your guests like penalties for late check-ins and base rate, you have to communicate them before a booking is secured.

I'm sure this doesn't quite seem exhaustive – I mean, we are talking about PRICING- the most important part of this piece! But don't worry, we'll go through it more deeply in the next section.

This is just an overview.

How to Make Your First Million Dollars With Airbnb

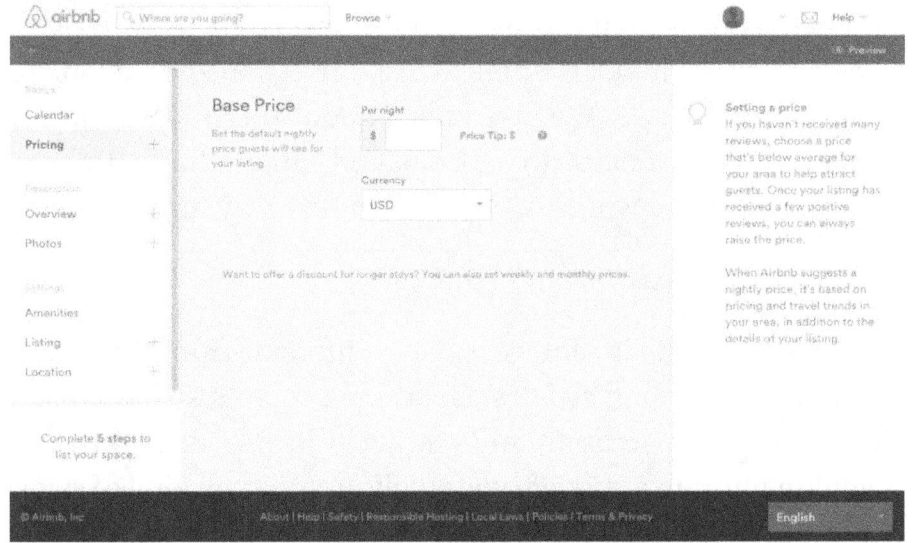

The overview

Title- As we both know, the title is your first impression, and it has to be very engaging to capture the attention while still being unique enough to depict your place accurately. You can try to use descriptive and nice adjectives to cushion your title.

Well, it's not as simple as that. For a title to be great, it has to:

Speak to your audience

Once again, think about your typical guest. Why is he/she visiting? We talked about this earlier. So I won't talk much about it. Assuming your target for this unit is couples, your unit should have suitable names to reflect that such as "Couple's Ultimate Getaway." As you can see, this will have to spark the interest of the viewers who travel as couples immediately.

Include the best features of your listing

How to Make Your First Million Dollars With Airbnb

Why do people want to stay at your house? What's your pad's best feature? These are some of the things you should look to include in the title. We also talked about this and anyway, it shouldn't be difficult. If you are targeting families with kids, how about using words like secure and homely in your title?

Use catchy words

An Airbnb title is not so much different from writing a headline for online articles. Good blog writers spend almost half their time creating and testing titles for their posts. It wouldn't hurt to approach your tagline with such kind of rigor. Instead of writing "a great apartment in a nice location," you could have something like "Elegant Hideaway | Close to your Desires." It does sound enticing- especially for couples- wouldn't you agree? Generally, avoid using ordinary words like *great, good,* and *nice* and consider more descriptive words that immediately paint a detailed image such as *modern, thrilling, spacious, rustic, eclectic,* and *historical.*

The summary- In 250 characters or less, you have to write a great summary to cover some of the major features of your listing.

Before we talk a bit about what you should include in your summary, I want you always to have one thing at the back of your mind: brevity. The devil is always in the details. Your summary should immediately answer your potential guests' questions preemptively. Some of the most important guest questions you have to answer include:

- How far is your property from the nearest bus stop/ train station/ airport?
- Is there a mall nearby to purchase any essentials?
- How are the beds? Your guests want to have a rough estimate of the number of people the unit can accommodate.
- Do you allow pets in the units?
- Are there any rules regarding partying, noise levels, or anything like that?

These are a few general questions that guests have. You should tailor your list to match your target group. Speaking of which, you should align your entire summary with your target audience.

Let's take an example.

If you're renting out your property to travelers, and it is located in a more culturally vibrant town area, you should include words that show off that particular aspect to this kind of guest. I would also advise any host to write their summaries, thinking "inside the unit" as well as "outside the unit." As an example, let's see an example that would be appealing to groups of people looking to relax in a place away from the busy city streets.

Inside the unit:

"Unwind in this cozy studio with gorgeous mountain views, free parking, and a pool ..."

How to Make Your First Million Dollars With Airbnb

Outside the unit:

"... all within walking distance to taverns, vintage cafés, and art venues."

Just avoid too much writing; it always looks daunting.

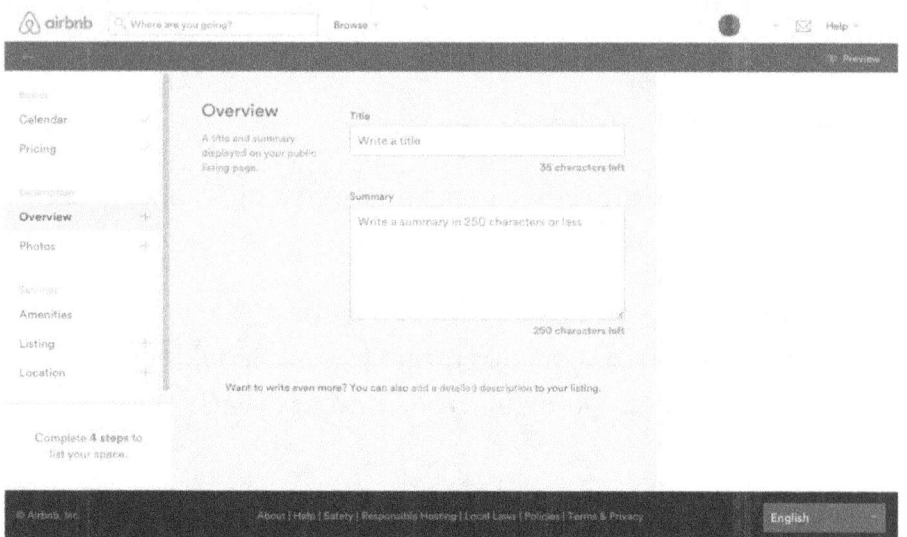

The pictures

By the time you get here, I assume that you already have great photos ready to be posted. While Airbnb allows you to add as many photos as you can, you should only add around 10. You don't want to overwhelm your potential guests and look like you're trying too hard. Nonetheless, even if you upload all ten of them, remember that the first three will always be the most important since they frame the window into your listing before users decide to click into your listing or not. Like I said earlier, pictures are everything, and that's why I emphasized on quality, tailor-made high-resolution images to market your listing. This is your chance to show off the most important parts of your property.

Airbnb also recommends using larger photos for the best resolution (1024 by 638px). So go ahead, choose your images carefully, and add them to the site.

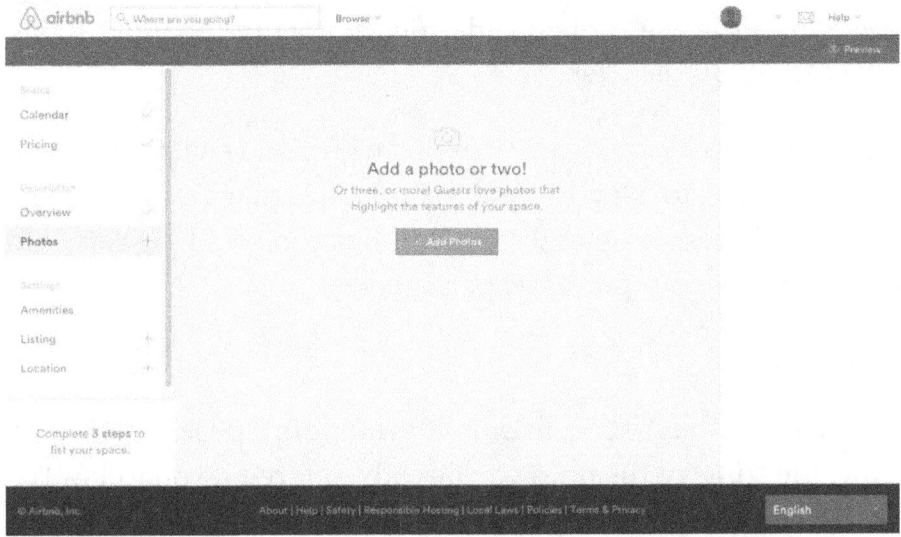

Amenities

As you will note, this section contains a long list of features ranging from common, extra rooms to home safety measures that you have to describe. At this point, you have the option of selecting from the available list of amenities; however, when the listing is created, you will be able to edit this part and add more or further details and descriptions. Just ensure you include all the appropriate features since some guests will definitely be swayed by a few extras or be uninterested when they don't see them.

For instance, these can be as simple as a first aid kit or some edibles. A first aid kit is not the most exciting accessory, but its provision is critical. For one, it enables your guests to take care of themselves in case they experience a minor accident, but perhaps more importantly, it sends them a critical message: that you've made their well-being a matter of priority. The latter (edibles), which may include things like a few snacks in the kitchen and a nice bottle of wine in the living room, can do the trick.

You can also be creative by placing a grill and coal in the yard, add a game to play (a deck of cards perhaps?) or cooking utensils. These seemingly small things can go a long way into maximizing your guests' experience.

Listing

Now enter the Airbnb listing information. These details may include some of the ones you already entered if you follow the steps properly. You make editions on all the items unless you're listing one room (which can be shared or private); in this case, you should pre-register the total number of bedrooms as 1.

Location

All you need to do here is input the location of your listing, and the whole Airbnb listing process will be complete. When you start typing your address, the site will suggest the rest of the details to auto-fill for accuracy and convenience. Once the location is entered, you will be prompted to add directions (with a box) and generate a section below with a notice of your local property laws for reference purposes. The public will not

How to Make Your First Million Dollars With Airbnb

be able to view the location indicated, which means that you should rest assured that you won't have your private information being circulated on the web. Instead, a circle will pop up on a map on your listing- at the bottom- to give you a good idea of your entire area and neighborhood.

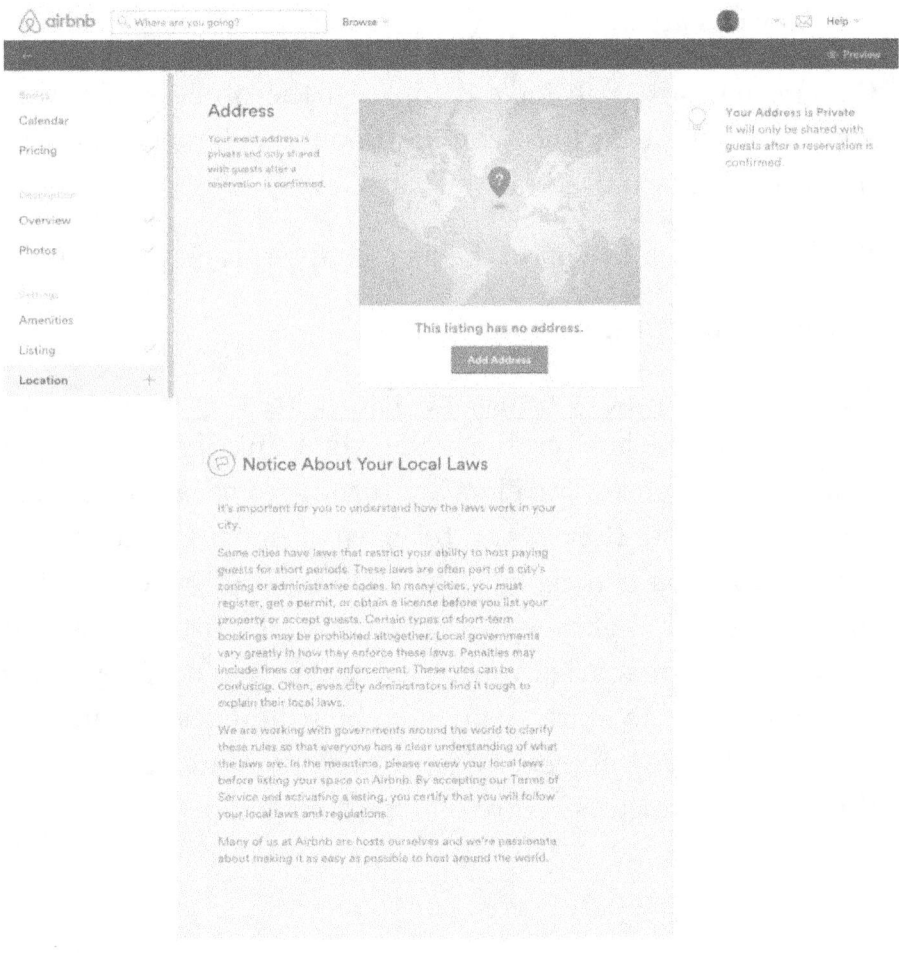

When you're done with this part and are satisfied with your listing, you're set to be published on the mighty Airbnb. You, however, have to remember that you have to be very honest in your description as it never takes long for the truth to be uncovered once guests arrive. Nonetheless, you can try spinning some features that aren't extremely appealing as much as possible- just to put your property out there in the best way possible.

Congratulations! You have completed the process of listing your property on Airbnb. You have done the largest chunk of the work, and what's left is very little.

But before you move on to the next chapter, remember to:

Optimize your host profile

To some potential guests, the listing of a property is as important as the host profile, and if you think about it, it does make a lot of sense. Travelers are turning to vacation rentals, mainly because they want to have a more personalized experience. You can replace the stale marketing seen in the modern hotel industry with a creative, well written, clear-cut Airbnb profile to market your property. A great profile picture is a good place to start. Also, talk about how passionate you are about hosting and serving people, and invite guests to go through your reviews before making a booking.

How To Price Your Unit

This part requires no introduction. It's the most challenging part and yet, arguably, the most important. Let's see how you can determine the price of your unit, starting with a step I had roughly mentioned in some parts of the book:

Gather the data about your local competition

Earlier on, we had mentioned that you have to look at what your competition is doing to know your position. When it comes to setting prices for your property, you have to understand the supply and demand dynamics in your local area at different times of the year, which you'll utilize to maximize your earning potential.

Let's first go back a couple of steps in this book. The price suggestion Airbnb provided to you when you were listing your property was calculated by taking into account a very limited number of factors. The factors considered are things like your location, the number of bathrooms and bedrooms, the quality of your property, the kind of amenities being offered to guests in your property as well as the total number of guests it can accommodate.

With such criteria, it may seem like they're covering a broad range of variables —enough to make you compare with other listings, but that's not true. Naturally, there are limits to the ability of Airbnb to get listings that can be compared to yours, without having more info about your place than what they ask for. You'll never find two listings that are the same despite the 'obvious' commonalities that may be there between them.

How to Make Your First Million Dollars With Airbnb

Your aim of researching your local competition is to know more about the comparable listings within your locale so that you have a good idea of the optimal amount of money you can charge for your unit at different times of the year.

In a bit, though, you'll have all the details you need about that, including how you can utilize the different important factors to determine the different prices. Just remember that the slightest mistake in pricing can lead to the failure of your Airbnb investment- especially if you're a new host.

So to start, draw a simple monthly table like this one:

MONTH	AVAILABLE LISTINGS	AVERAGE NIGHTLY COST	NEW AVERAGE NIGHTLY COST	
			NEW COST	WITH 30% REDUCTION
JAN				
FEB				
MAR				
APR				
MAY				
JUN				
JUL				
AUG				
SEP				
OCT				
NOV				
DEC				
AVERAGE:				

How to Make Your First Million Dollars With Airbnb

After that, step into the shoes of a guest who's looking to find a place on Airbnb similar to yours. To do that, get onto Airbnb and start searching as though you were a guest, trying to get a place within your neighborhood. Be very specific when you enter the location. For instance, instead of New York, enter Bronx, New York.

For the dates, enter '14th January' as the day of check-in and '16th January' as the check-out day"- i.e., the middle of the month.

When the search results are displayed, work through the various search filters displayed to you- these should be above the thumbnails of the listing and beneath the search bar located at the top.

Choose all the filters that are applicable to your listing. For instance, if you wish to list the entire 3-bedroom, 2-bathroom apartment, then choose the tab labeled "Entire Home" for the Room Type and "2+ bathrooms" as well as "3+ bedrooms" for the 'rooms and beds.'

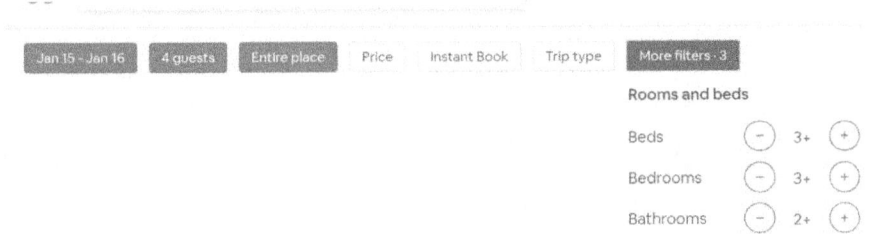

You should also choose any facilities, amenities, or anything else that can assist in categorizing your listing with other similar listings. You'll be presented with results, but what you should be interested in are two important information pieces:

How to Make Your First Million Dollars With Airbnb

1. *The average price per night*

When you click on the price filter, you'll see the average price per night. The example below shows that the price is $508. Nonetheless, it's clear that this amount also includes what we can refer to as "outlier" listings on the right end of the displayed price range graph (the expensive end). The 'outlier' listings are a lot more expensive than the rest of the listings to the left.

We'll, therefore, want to leave out outlier listings- these can be both cheap and expensive since they are skewing the average price per night in the neighborhood disproportionately.

Here is how to go about it:

Drag the circle for a minimum price to the left side towards the low price end of the graph to remove any cheaper outliers, and for the maximum price, drag the circle that's on the right-hand side on the upper end of the graph to remove the expensive outliers. The price range with the outliers is as follows:

$10 - $1000+

The average total price is $508

How to Make Your First Million Dollars With Airbnb

The price range without the outliers is as follows:

$227 - $899

The average total price is $508

You'll now calculate the nightly cost as follows:

(The new lowest price + the new highest price) / 2

Using the example above, we can see that the new lowest price is $227 and the new highest price is $899. This, therefore, means that you can calculate the new nightly average cost as follows:

($227+$899)/ 2 = $563

The number of listings available

Airbnb will tell you the number of listings that match your search with all the filters you specified (this will be located at the bottom of every search results page). In the example here, Airbnb responded by saying the total number of listings available are 109 rentals. From this, we can gather the following:

How to Make Your First Million Dollars With Airbnb

The first thing is that in your locale, there are about 109 listings comparable to yours in the middle of January.

It's also clear that their average nightly cost is $563.

You can now try populating the first row's two columns – that is for January – of your table with the figures. Don't mind the last two columns for now.

MONTH	AVAILABLE LISTINGS	AVERAGE NIGHTLY COST	NEW AVERAGE NIGHTLY COST	
			NEW COST	WITH 30% REDUCTION
JAN	109	$563		

You'll have to do that 12 times, each time representing each month of the year. This way, you'll ensure the prices you determine accurately account for the variation across the different months. This, in particular, can affect the locations that typically have broad seasonal travel variations throughout the year. You can do this by updating the dates of your search on the site to the 15th day of each month, and repeat the same for February through December.

How to Make Your First Million Dollars With Airbnb

When you repeat this process 11 more times, you should end up with a table with the first two columns complete. You want to see something close to this:

How to Make Your First Million Dollars With Airbnb

MONTH	AVAILABLE LISTINGS	AVERAGE NIGHTLY COST	NEW AVERAGE NIGHTLY COST	
			NEW COST	WITH 30% REDUCTION
JAN	109	$563		
FEB	92	$580		
MAR	79	$557		
APR	88	$547		
MAY	84	$560		
JUN	73	$585		
JUL	76	$575		
AUG	62	$533		
SEP	59	$552		
OCT	60	$548		
NOV	56	$528		
DEC	61	$548		

Now try working out the average in the bottom row. Just add the figures for all the months and divide the result by 12.

MONTH	AVAILABLE LISTINGS	AVERAGE NIGHTLY COST	NEW AVERAGE NIGHTLY COST	
			NEW COST	WITH 30% REDUCTION
AVERAGE	75	$556		

The next thing you should do is move away from just understanding your competition and start determining your optimal price per night for each month of the year. You can do this by making pricing changes that reflect the demand and supply of the available listings at different periods of the year.

How to Make Your First Million Dollars With Airbnb

To make your work simpler, you can use the following framework to make these manual adjustments:

The adjustments, using our example, will look something like this:

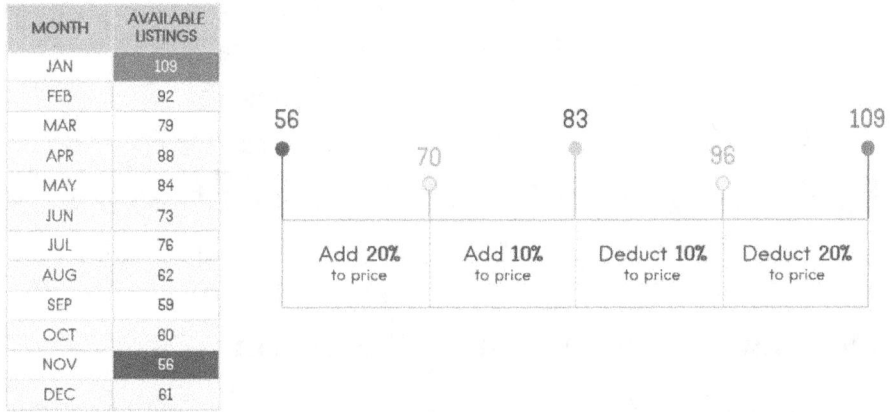

You are now armed with the necessary figures to populate the table's *new cost* column. It should, therefore, look something like this:

How to Make Your First Million Dollars With Airbnb

MONTH	AVAILABLE LISTINGS	AVERAGE NIGHTLY COST	NEW AVERAGE NIGHTLY COST	
			NEW COST	WITH 30% REDUCTION
JAN	109	$563	$563 - 20% = $450	
FEB	92	$580	$580 - 10% = $522	
MAR	79	$557	$557 + 10% = $613	
APR	88	$547	$547 - 10% = $492	
MAY	84	$560	$560 - 10% = $504	
JUN	73	$585	$585 + 10% = $644	
JUL	76	$575	$575 + 10% = $633	
AUG	62	$533	$533 + 20% = $640	
SEP	59	$552	$552 + 20% = $662	
OCT	60	$548	$548 + 20% = $658	
NOV	56	$528	$528 + 20% = $634	
DEC	61	$548	$548 + 20% = $658	
AVERAGE:	75	$556	$593	

Move away from the generalized pricing

You can have one year-round price for your property just like many properties out there, but it'll almost always represent a missed opportunity.

In this light, this step will give you the chance to use the information you discovered through researching to make sound monthly adjustments to the default price per night -all year round. Before you update your monthly prices, you should also consider making informed, strategic discounts to the amount you arrived at from the previous step.

How to Make Your First Million Dollars With Airbnb

The reason is simple: the guests typically feel more comfortable booking with hosts who have a proven track record. You want to increase your options for getting around this problem since you're a new host.

As I mentioned earlier, you can offer lower prices to attract guests, but it is advisable to lower your prices only until a time when you've established a good track record on Airbnb- which is when you'll be able to go back to the normal prices.

As a new host, you can discount your prices between a range of between 20 and 40 percent, until you have at least 5- 10 guest reviews. Soon, you'll learn that these discounts will prove a little price to pay to boost the pace of your success. The extra profits that you will make subsequently will cover (usually over) all the short-term losses you incurred on your way there.

Let's assume you implemented a 30 percent discount to the last example; this means that your new temporarily-reduced numbers will be similar to this:

How to Make Your First Million Dollars With Airbnb

MONTH	AVAILABLE LISTINGS	AVERAGE NIGHTLY COST	NEW AVERAGE NIGHTLY COST	
			NEW COST	WITH 30% REDUCTION
JAN	109	$563	$450	$450 - 30% = $315
FEB	92	$580	$522	$522 - 30% = $365
MAR	79	$557	$613	$613 - 30% = $429
APR	88	$547	$492	$492 - 30% = $344
MAY	84	$560	$504	$504 - 30% = $353
JUN	73	$585	$644	$644 - 30% = $451
JUL	76	$575	$633	$633 - 30% = $443
AUG	62	$533	$640	$640 - 30% = $448
SEP	59	$552	$662	$662 - 30% = $463
OCT	60	$548	$658	$658 - 30% = $461
NOV	56	$528	$634	$634 - 30% = $444
DEC	61	$548	$658	$658 - 30% = $461
AVERAGE:	75	$556	$593	$415

In the example above, you can see that after applying the temporarily discounted rate of 30 percent, your new average cost per night for the whole year is $415. For January, the cost is $315. You may also have to update your calendar's pricing to reflect these average cost figures- which include the 30% temporary reductions if you're a new host- for all the months of the year.

To update the prices, log in to Airbnb, and in the hosting mode, choose 'Calendar' from the top menu. Select all the dates of the month- for instance, 1st January to 31st January. Input your updated nightly rate- for instance, $315 for January- in the nightly price input box and save.

How to Make Your First Million Dollars With Airbnb

Selected dates

Tue, 1st Jan → Thu, 31st Jan

Availability

Available ●

Blocked ○

Nightly price

$ 315

Repeat this process for all the remaining months of the year.

You've now been able to shift from a generalized or one-size-fits-all strategy of setting your price to one that optimizes your monthly earning potential.

Raising the prices when there's a high demand

So far, you've seen how possible it is to create a more granular strategy of pricing that reflects your capacity to command different prices for the different months of the year. But you can still be able to take this step further.

As you know, there are certain periods (days or weeks) where your local area or city is more popular than other times throughout the year. Good examples here include conferences, sporting events, and conventions. With Airbnb, you can create custom pricing for special dates like these.

During such times, you will be able to charge more for your place than at other times of the year. To do so, though, you'll

How to Make Your First Million Dollars With Airbnb

have to have researched key events taking place in your local area or city to identify what they are and when they're taking place. Like honey to bees, these events will draw in more travelers and tourists who are going to require places to stay- that means that the demand will be pushed up and the supply (lodges, hotels, Airbnb units, etc.) will stay fixed. In other words, you'll have a chance to charge more for your place.

A simple Google search will reveal all the times when this will be possible. For instance, you could search for *Key events in New York 2020* or *annual events in New York*. You'll get something like this:

Date	Event
11 – 18 February	New York Fashion Week
17 – 28 April	Tribeca Film Festival
21 – 26 June	Gay Pride Week
9 June	Museum Mile Festival
8 – 24 August	New York International Fringe Festival
25 August – 8 September	U.S. Open
11 – 21 September	Feast of San Gennaro
6 – 9 October	New York Comic-Con
6 November	TCS New York City Marathon
27 November	Macy's Thanksgiving Day Parade

You should then try to compile 10 -15 important events that you believe would most likely affect the supply of short-term accommodation options for areas within and outside places where you live.

Just remember that custom monthly or weekly prices will override the regular monthly, weekly and nightly prices, as well as any custom nightly prices you could have saved on your calendar.

If you're not sure how much more you could charge for special events, you could try checking out the extra amount of money hotels are charging for the same period. You definitely won't be copying their exact prices, but you may want to replicate the same price pattern increases for the amounts you're charging already.

It's very important to be aware of events happening in your area as often as possible to be able to stay on top of the game and make your custom prices in good time. Potential guests preparing to attend such events always lock in their accommodation before the actual date of the event. If you raise your prices after they book, you'll have a problem. As a general rule, aim to lock-in your price increases for important events between 6 and 12 months before the start of the actual event. This is the reason why making early event research is important.

Note:

Before you increase your prices for a specific event, you'll need to ensure that the kind of guests likely to attend it are ones who would be interested in your place. For instance, if you're having shared rooms located in a neighborhood that's not glamorous on the outskirts of New York City (where the event is taking place), you really shouldn't consider a custom price increase.

Selected dates

Mon, 11th Fel → Mon, 18th Fe

Availability

Available ●

Blocked ○

Nightly price

$ 200

Offer long-term discounts

You should also think about offering monthly or weekly discounts as an incentive for potential guests who need a long-term accommodation option. Sometimes, charging less on Airbnb can generate more profit for you than charging more. It does sound counter-intuitive I know- since you may lose a couple of dollars in each booking, but it may afford you longer-term, loyal guests. This is particularly true for the guests who are open to the idea of extending their stay.

Let's take a look at two scenarios as an example. One of them has a weekly discount offer, and the other doesn't have any weekly discount offer:

How to Make Your First Million Dollars With Airbnb

	Discount Offered	No Discount Offered
Nightly rental price	$100	
Weekly discount	10%	None
Number of 1 night stays	1	
Number of 2 night stays	2	
Number of Weekly stays	3	2
Monthly income	($100 x 1) + ($200 x 2) + ($700 x 3 - 10%) = $2,390	($100 x 1) + ($200 x 2) + ($700 x 2) = $1,900

When you are offered a 10 percent weekly discount as the host, you can attract one more weekly stay, and this ends up netting you an extra $490 in your monthly revenue.

We both know that discounts entice everyone and more people are therefore more likely to consider places offering lower rates.

Adding extra fees

Weekend charges

With Airbnb, you are allowed to increase your fee a bit during the weekends since potential guests travel more during the weekend, creating more demand during these days.

You should, however, reserve the weekend pricing when your listing starts getting an increase in travel during the weekends. However, if your property gets a consistent inflow of guests throughout the week, having higher prices (during the weekend) may come as a disincentive for the guests who may be considering your unit when there are cheaper alternatives. You need to consider that.

When you enable this price increase, it will replace the price per night for Friday and Saturday.

So, by how much should you increase your price?

There is no prescribed figure that you can use when you want to increase your weekend prices. Nonetheless, you can implement a 10 -15 percent increase on your regular weekday rate. If you want more accurate data, you can do a quick search on Airbnb to find out what other similar listings in your area are charging for weekends.

Additional guests

You also have the freedom to charge a nightly fee of a reservation for any additional guests. All you need to do is define the total number of people required in your unit before the feel for extra guests sets in and specify the amount for each extra guest.

The benefit of having this fee is that it will assist you to offer your property at a lower price and only charge more for bookings that typically require a bigger guest count. This way, it has the potential of making your place seem cheaper to smaller parties who want a place to stay. The main disadvantage of this arrangement is that it is very difficult to enforce in your absence at the check-in to confirm the total number of guests who are arriving for the booking. Some guests have been reported to interpreting this fee as an indication that the host is overbearing- as you know, this may be a huge disincentive.

You, therefore, have to weigh up the likely pros and cons of incorporating this approach to your investment before making your final decision. As you do so, consider your target groups and the kind of space you are offering to them.

I believe that by now, you have your pricing right and are ready to move on to the next step.

Here's what you should do next:

Market Your Property

Create a social media presence

One of the best things you should think of tackling right off the bat is managing and promoting social media accounts for your listing. Think of establishing a cohesive brand around your listing- which includes a unique, catchy name and logo and ensuring that the brand name stays consistent across all the platforms.

So, what should you share?

The most obvious content here is pictures of your vacation rental. Begin by posting nice photos of the interior of your listing and work your way to the outside. Airbnb's social media accounts can include anything from pictures of restaurants and local bars to natural attractions around your property. You shouldn't get discouraged if each post you make doesn't generate as many likes or engagement as you wish to have- actually, the fact that you're managing a social media account gives potential guests the impression that you're serious, which instills in them confidence and trust that is required to hit the booking button.

Even so, social media doesn't limit you to making posts on your page. You can also join vacation rental forums on social media. These are places specifically created for hosts to interact with other Airbnb hosts as well as property managers. Here, you'll undoubtedly gain real, tried, and tested insights on the best way to manage your listings.

You don't have to go as far as creating a blog for your Airbnb listing (you should consider it though); you should make a story out of it. Draw in potential guests looking for certain experiences by using your social media stories, and you'll get more bookings than you expect. Whatever you do, though, never forget your target audience.

Work with a blogger or journalist

This strategy works well if taken as a long-term growth strategy. As you know, lifestyle bloggers who have many social media followers; and journalists as well can attract many people to your property.

There are many ways of attracting the attention of these professionals, but one of the best ones is letting them stay at your property for free so that they're able to review it and post about it. Contact them directly and explain your offer carefully. Most of them would be willing to do this as long as your listing features a significant number of reviews. So, if you can dedicate outbound marketing work, you can try and team up with high-profile journalists, bloggers, and influencers to assist you in promoting your vacation rental. Research people within your locale who have a significant following in travel spaces, and then create an engaging template to invite them to stay at your place for a night all for free. Inform them that, in return, they have to post something on their account praising your listing. Remember that this can be as simple as a tweet, blog post, a YouTube video, a picture on Instagram, or anything on the network they prefer.

Create a referral program

Many industries largely depend on referral business. While short-term rentals don't traditionally fit in this category, it doesn't mean you can't bring onboard some great promotional offers. In fact, Airbnb has its own in-house referral program. You can offer your guests between 10 and 20 percent off their stay at your place when they successfully refer someone to your property. You can also consider operating this transaction outside Airbnb by making payments through companies like PayPal.

Come up with a unique URL to promote your listing

If you have a unique angle in mind that you can use to promote your listing, a good example being its locale, architecture, or amenities, you can create a unique URL. This makes it easier to track the traffic to your listing on Airbnb; it's also quite easy for guests to remember. You definitely might have considered URL (it's pretty basic), but you can take it to the next step of purchasing a domain that redirects people to your Airbnb listing. This only takes a couple of minutes; moreover, at least you'll have a domain that is easy to remember that you can share with prospective guests.

Let's take a look at one example. You have an apartment in Bronx district of New York. You can go to a domain registry site such as Hostgator, domain.com, or GoDaddy to register a URL www.bronxapartment.com. After owning that domain name, you'll be able to set up a redirect so that you're able to forward the URL to your standard listing on Airbnb. It's very easy and it rarely takes more than 15 minutes!

Have your name in your area's tourism websites

How to Make Your First Million Dollars With Airbnb

These include hostels and hotels websites. Get your properties listed with these websites since they are always trusted resources for visitors who come from out of your town. Sooner than you think, you might enjoy a huge boost in your bookings.

Make flyers and business cards

If the internet is your main medium for promoting your listings, you shouldn't overlook the offline advertising methods. Make flyers and business cards and strategically leave them at local businesses most frequented by tourists within your area. These could be local events and restaurants.

If you have time or travel often, you can give out business cards to folks you meet and even invite them personally to stay at your Airbnb each time they think of visiting your area. Nothing beats the deeper connection that's established when advertisers meet their potential clients in person. This may help you outdo the Airbnb competition.

At this point, you know how to invest in Airbnb with your own (or acquired) property, and with someone else's property (through arbitrage). You've also done the math and set the figures and even marketed your property.

So where do you go from here?

Well- you could do what most Airbnb millionaires are doing: add more and more properties to your overall list of investments (and it's very advisable to do so). But that could take time and prove to be very costly.

But there's another way.

You could add another low-cost Airbnb investment strategy to your repertoire, which is being a manager. As you manage your properties, you could also manage a few others- owned by other people (alongside your own) and generate real income that only real entrepreneurs net.

As I explained earlier in the book, it's not easy to acquire property in the current economy, so chances are you'll start your process without owning any property at all. But you are eager to create and expand your portfolio while incurring the lowest upfront costs and risk possible, right? I believe you do- so let me introduce to you another less risky investment strategy for people who don't own any property:

Being An Airbnb Property Manager (Strategy #3)

Also known as co-hosting, you can increase your income on Airbnb by becoming an Airbnb property manager.

This method enables you to make money running other people's Airbnb properties without investing anything significant while still scaling a lot quicker than with most other models. As a business person managing short-term properties, you'll be in constant communication with the homeowner, their guests, and staff.

Being a manager is great, especially if you also decide to go the rental arbitrage route (which is arguably a higher income-generating model than being a property manager) since it's volatile. You want to protect the integrity and security of your overall investment, don't you? I mean, for instance, you never know when the regulations regarding the previously discussed models will change and force you to switch to longer-term rental models.

With the Airbnb property management business model, your overall investment is hedged against such an event since your name is not the one on the contract associated with the property. Typically, the property owner is allowed to do what they want with their property – if they decide to list it as a short-term rental, there are few regulations to stop them from doing so.

What's more, if regulations are created and they happen to undermine short-term rentals, you'll have a lot less to lose. All you'll need to do is find yourself another property owner and start managing their property.

As the Airbnb property manager, you'll be the one responsible for paying the rent, maintaining the units, utilities, and so forth- basically, pretty much all the things you'll be doing as regards to the management of your properties.

How to become an Airbnb property manager

First of all, you have to understand the industry. This is why it's important to start this business after a while of managing your units. Don't start immediately. When you've set up a fully-fledged business with your properties, and are comfortable with your investment as a host, you'll be ready to hop onto the business of managing other people's properties.

Think about it; this will not only put you out there as an experienced host who knows what he/she is doing but will also prepare you meticulously for all the issues that may come up.

Create your business plan

The next thing you need to do is come up with an Airbnb business plan. This is as simple as planning out how you're going to work with your cleaners, the Airbnb property management you are going to use, the kind of properties you are going to manage, and how you are going to price your Airbnb listings. Do you plan on managing everything yourself, or are you going to hire a team? Remember that as you scale, you'll have to take on a couple of team members- if just for cleaning.

What you're doing here is no different from creating a small company, so you'll need a clear business plan to go with it. Just ensure that in your business plan, you account for any third-party vendors you'll require to assist you in solving any problems your clients may experience. Some of these issues include the following:

- Cleaners and backup cleaners
- HVAC repair services
- Plumbing and electrical services
- Pest control
- Pool cleaning services
- Any other emergency support

When your business plan is ready...

Come up with a maintenance management system

Short-term rentals entail guests repeatedly checking in and out, and therefore, the process of managing these rentals will involve you, the manager, in checking the property before your guests arrive and immediately after they leave. You also have to perform routine maintenance of the property to ensure the units are in perfect condition all the time. This is very important to ensure the satisfaction of your client and your guests as well. But this can only be simple for so long.

Take the following scenario as an example:

Your guest in a 2-bedroom villa decides to check out one day before the expected day and requires more towels, and another one in a condo that's 20 minutes away from the city center is complaining about the Wi-Fi. These are just two people; you could be having 90 guests to deal with! With more bookings comes a bigger need to coordinate between multiple properties at various checkout times and with people that never leave or arrive at the agreed time.

Automation

You need help, and that's where automation comes in. You need to sync calendars across more than one listing, and share the calendar with your team members; a good automated Airbnb property management system can help you with that. Basically, a software that can do the following (apart from having a multi-calendar dashboard) is what you should be looking for:

- Integrating your listings to streamline operations

How to Make Your First Million Dollars With Airbnb

- Easing the process of keeping track of communication with different guests

- Automating that particular communication

- Keeping all the various Airbnb accounts in one place

Let's take a quick look at the features that various automated property management software usually have -to enable you to find one that suits your needs.

Remember that as the number of your listings grows, you have to remain at the top of your calendar to know the times when people are checking in and out. Standard management software will update the calendar across different channels automatically, which is particularly important when it comes to working with different team members responsible for different properties.

Good software examples (for a central calendar for bookings) include the following:

- Your Porter

- **Lodgify**

- Hostfully

- Smartbnb

- iGMS

When it comes to cleaning and overall team management tasks, the same software listed above can help- though a bit differently. The systems are, however, generally great at delegating tasks to workers who can view, accept, and, when completed, mark them accordingly.

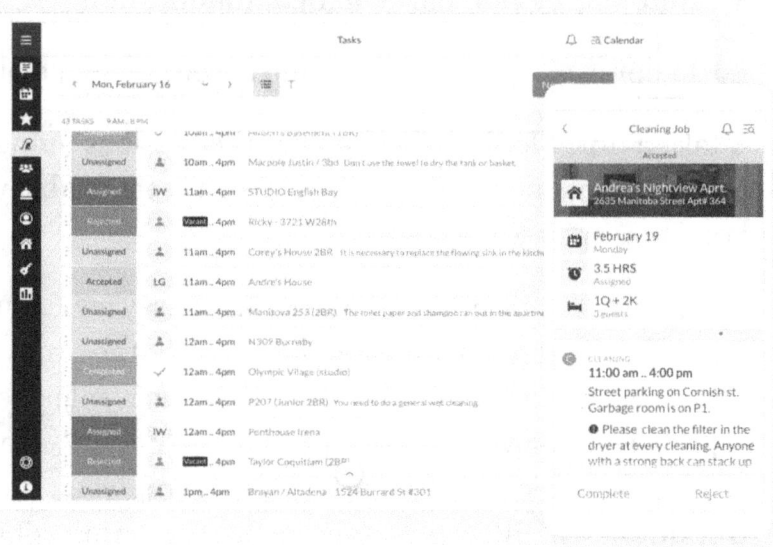

- Your Porter: Offers email and SMS notifications of tasks, as well as push notifications when the tasks are completed. It also offers weekly and monthly task overviews as well as a shared calendar- though with limited access.

- Hostfully: this one offers fully automated task creation and delegates jobs or tasks to service providers and teams as well (via triggers and templates).

- Smartbnb: creates and assigns tasks like cleaning, check-in/check-out jobs automatically, and also sends automated notifications to teammates through SMS or email; it also keeps them updated with iCal feeds.

How to Make Your First Million Dollars With Airbnb

- **iGMS**: this is an advanced cleaning and team project management platform that is both automated and designed for Real-time feedback. It allows you to set the roles and auto-assign tasks.

Next up is automated guest communication.

Guest experience	Messaging rules
Overview	
Messaging rules	
Before booking	New booki... / New inquiry / All / 1
Before check-in	
Staying	New booki... / New inquiry / All / 1
After check-out	New pre-a... / New pre-approval / All / 1
Review rules	
Questions	New reque... / New request to book / All / 1
Custom codes	
Canned responses	Reply to Pa... / Parking / All / 1

This is probably one of the most important parts of the guests' experience and is always one of the most tedious tasks for the host. Unfortunately, most hosts have to go through the outdated process of cutting and posting of messages for every guest they receive even though it's a very annoying, not to mention tedious, especially when the host scales up.

Lucky for you, most automated Airbnb management software comes with integrated automated messaging functions. This saves time and improves your response time since you get to answer guests instantly, something that means that your listings' ranking will improve, which translates to more listings, but many more messages. And you can utilize them to go past the standard message flow.

How to Make Your First Million Dollars With Airbnb

For instance, Smartbnb can allow you to configure your answer to some of your guests' random questions in a non-disingenuous manner. If you're the type that can get worried about having some 'bot' responding to your guests, there are great options for you. For instance, you can set your software up to respond to common questions- for example, if one guest writes to you with the name 'cat' in their message, you can relay an automated message consisting of answers to any questions you've ever received about cats. This way, you'll likely cover the question and save time. The other option you'll have is to limit your automatic answers to questions on topics that are usually very straightforward, like parking, Wi-Fi, and pets, and then answer the rest of the questions manually.

All the software listed above can assist you with this task pretty effectively.

So, how about price management?

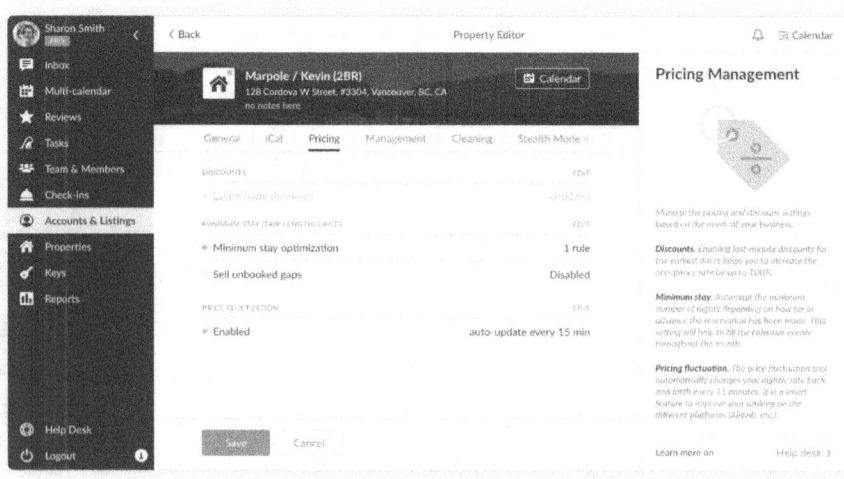

Your pricing strategy should not be the same across booking channels. It's useful to have a property management software that has a tool that can simplify this for you. For example, *Your Porter* software takes the host's smart prices from Airbnb and sends them to *Booking.com* after adjusting with your tailored markup rate.

- **Your Porter:** it mark-ups, pushes your prices, and keeps your Booking.com prices updated according to your Airbnb rules. It is integrated with all the key smart pricing tools such as BeyondPricing, Wheelhouse, and PriceLabs (These are management systems that can enable you to create smart pricing rules for different properties and even use past data to optimize your current pricing).

- **Hostfully:** offers sophisticated price management and total control over *multi-channel* pricing.

- **Lodgify:** this one works across all channels, contains API (application programming interface) Integrations with Outswitch and PriceLabs dynamic pricing tools; it also functions well across all channels.

- **Smartbnb:** Pushes prices to Airbnb and HomeAway (a rental marketplace). It's also integrated with PriceLabs.

- **iGMS:** this is a smart toolkit pricing management that you can modify right from the calendar. It pushes pricing to Airbnb and HomeAway.

We also have another equally important task: guest review management.

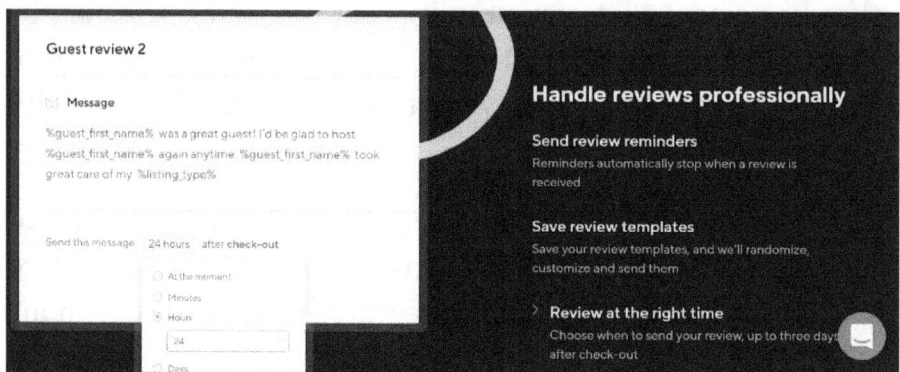

The automated property management software is another great feature you need to look out for. Hosts know very well that the more reviews they write, the more they get back, and the more reviews they get, the higher the rank and the more listings they get. Therefore, it would be great to automate guest reviews to go out at certain times during the checkouts, and this will be another task you'll have checked in your to-do list.

- **Your Porter:** contains 60 templates you can choose from for automatic review guests.

- **Lodgify:** doesn't contain any such feature.

- **Hostfully:** doesn't contain any such feature.

- **Smartbnb:** comes with automatic positive guest reviews according to the templates attributed indiscriminately. You can also get into the 'bad review mode' which allows you to send your negative review within 20 seconds before the review window closes- this means that guests won't have a chance to hit back.

- **iGMS:** comes with automated guest reviews which are set according to your templates.

After setting up your property management systems, the next thing you should do is find opportunities.

Looking for hosts and owners

Unless you're planning on knocking doors seeking clients, there are suitable ways and tools that are already at your disposal to track down potential hosts and owners looking for management or a co-host.

Tap your contacts

Managing your properties will make you an entrepreneur of sorts, and you'll increase the number of contacts you have of people related or affiliated to the short-term rental industry. At this point, you can call and talk to them about the possibility of assisting them (if they own Airbnb properties) or people they know who need a property manager.

Dig through the inter-webs

It is possible to find someone looking for a vocational rental manager on job boards just by taking your time on the web. Actually, such job boards could serve as a great place for you to list your availability. You could also consider checking on more industry-specific websites such as Airhosta. Airhosta is a website that matches potential property managers who need help with their listings and potential co-hosts.

Utilize the business blogging space

One of the best ways of appealing to owners is to let them know about your quality services through a blog. Create a blog and write about how to solve various property management problems, especially those related to Airbnb. In the eyes of Google, blogging is a very effective way of keeping your website up-to-date. The reason is simple: each time you post, it's interpreted as an extra indexed page on your website. In other words, by posting such information, you create an extra opportunity for you to show up in the search engines and redirect traffic to your website, increasing your chances of being found even more.

Be professional and land the gig

You now know where to start your search and get yourself some attention. The next step is making sure that when you begin exploring these avenues, you polish yourself to look the part and have yourself a great sales pitch. You aim to sell your skills as a co-host or vacation rental manager. Your preparedness and professionalism matter here.

So, in this case:

Create a proposal and show off

Since you'll be having some experience as a host yourself (by the time you get to this level), you'll be able to prove in detail that you know what you do and can handle assisting anyone owning any property, and run the show as an expert.

In your pitch, show your prospects that you have plans for:

- Fluid check-in and check-out procedures
- All the guest inquiries and general communication
- Emergencies
- Turnover cleaning
- Maintenance and upkeep

I am merely scratching the surface here; you need to be very prepared to show your best side. This leads me to the next point:

Focus on your uniqueness- what sets you apart?

Vacation rental management is a fairly old practice, and today, it's almost like everyone is getting into the business. You'll, therefore, need to have something that makes you different —or even better- than your competition. Think hard about what you can offer and be confident about it. It's likely going to be your highest selling point.

Charge your services reasonably (though competitively)

In most cases, vacation rental managers and co-hosts get a certain fixed percentage of the actual host's secured rental rate. This is often between 10 and 25 percent.

It may be quite tricky to set your rate because you want to avoid underselling yourself, yet trying to avoid overselling yourself at the same time. Some important considerations you can make are your experience and the unique points that you can offer and set yourself a rate.

You can also consider coming up with a tiered option as well to afford your host a little more flexibility. If your guests stay longer, for instance, you could negotiate a lower cut, perhaps? Eventually, you have to do what you think is best for you and be confident that what you are getting is truly worth what you think your services are truly worth.

Last but not least, automate financial reporting.

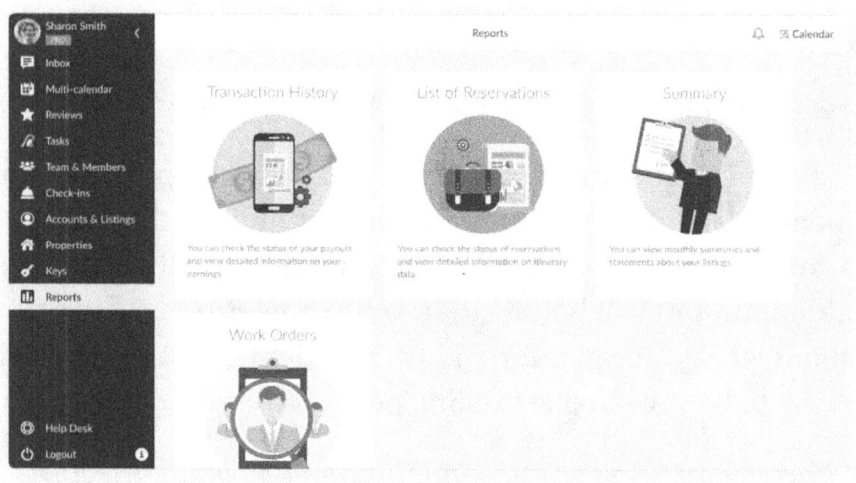

With multiple listings under your management, it means that you're a professional who has to stay at the top of his/her finances. It would serve you well to have a financial reporting well integrated into your short-term rental property management software. This will ensure you track income and the expenses well and ensure you remain on track.

- **Your Porter:** gives you a detailed report containing the price breakdowns from all the channels

- **Hostfully:** it presents to you your conversion rate, occupancy rate by property, revenue from the net bookings, and is integrated with Quickbooks- basically, all the analytics and reports.

- **Lodgify:** it majors on the transaction reports; it also allows you to connect it to your accounts system.

- **Smartbnb:** enables you to track over 40 metrics, which include messaging, financial, and reviews with dashboards and reports that you can customize.

- **iGMS:** Creates professional reports that contain detailed overviews of the transactions, finances, reservations, and work orders.

I think you get the idea, so I don't need to bore you with further details on automation. As we move on, let's consider the fact that even with automation, things can get tough, especially if you decide to take care of things by yourself. And it doesn't matter whether you're managing your properties, other people's properties, or a combination of both. This kind of business is a demanding prospect. Therefore, there are several tasks you should consider outsourcing. While you can analyze all the tasks running an Airbnb company involves and determine which ones to outsource, there are a few that most hosts generally find necessary to outsource. These are discussed in the next chapter below.

Outsourcing

Social media

One of the things we noted that you have to do after setting up your business is making your units appear more and more attractive to prospects. We talked about marketing on social media as one of the strategies you should incorporate as part of your campaign. However, with so much on your hands, social media management can prove an onerous task because of the obvious tasks (e.g., design and follow-up activities) it involves.

As you scale up, you'll need a social media manager.

A social media manager will be managing your online presence and letting you focus on other, more sensitive things in your business. A professional social media manager understands the internet well, knows where the people are, and so much more that is important to increase your bookings. He/she can map out a great plan for you on how to make the most of your listings to maximize their earnings.

Not convinced? Here are some of the ways an outsourced social media managers can convert your listings' views into guaranteed bookings:

Creative writing- a good social media manager is skilled in writing and can craft highly engaging posts for your listings. People look for these kinds of people's content to learn about the different places to see, stay in, visit, as well as the activities they can do to enjoy their time anywhere in the world. With the knack for writing that appeals to potential guests, such a professional can plan a marketing campaign that is sure to increase engagement and bookings.

Creative multimedia content- a social media manager is also to edit pictures and curate them nicely on your page. They have the experience and knowledge necessary to make the most recent digital marketing trends work for your listings- something you might not be able to do by yourself. They can also enhance how potential guests see your listings by creating informative videos of your property and ultimately, offering your guests a total feel of how it's like to be inside your home.

Customer service- you'll agree with me that good customer experience means quality service. A social media manager will assist you to keep track of reviews and use them to build the relationship between you and your customers. They'll do so by ensuring that you and your brand are clearly communicated. That's not all; such experts have access to different tools that can assist in monitoring conversations about your listings, fielding queries, and offering swift responses to questions and feedback.

Analysis of clicks and bookings- after you create content, promote your listing, and tend to your customers, it's very important to establish a measure of how successful your marketing efforts are. Outsourced social media managers are known for their ability to make good analyses of demographics (in this case, those who view your listings) and using them to tweak (your) strategies. For example, the social media manager you've outsourced work to can track what worked in your marketing model, and what failed. With this information, it's easier to turn the gathered data into informed guidelines and recommendations for improvement.

Where to find a good social media manager

It's actually very easy to outsource a good social media manager. One of the best places you can visit to get the perfect social media manager for you is a managed outsourcing firm known as [HOPLA](). Most successful hosts never have to worry about how to promote their listings on social media; they get the right person and worry about building a minibar and making their Airbnb dreams come true.

The next task you should outsource is:

Airbnb cleaning

You know that when you rent a unit on Airbnb, you should provide guests with a welcoming place to stay. Airbnb cleaning is, therefore, a must, and shouldn't be anything other than perfect.

It's possible to choose to take care of the cleaning yourself- by hiring a few workers to get the job done and so forth- but remember that as you scale, even managing the few workers, you'll have might be a problem. Actually, hosts who do this job themselves are often the ones owning smaller, fewer properties that don't demand a lot of administration. You should think of outsourcing early enough before circumstances force you to do so. Remember that there is a person/company out there specialized and committed to ensuring any property is pristine, and that's all they do.

Here're a couple of reasons why you need to consider outsourcing cleaning services:

It crosses one stressing factor off your list

Apart from being time-consuming, managing a property can be nerve-wracking. You have a long list of things to do- and this book, so far, has given a glimpse of what I'm talking about. It would make you more productive to give yourself one less issue to worry about- especially if it's something less sensitive, yet critical to your Airbnb business.

Your units will be cleaned to the best standards

Like I implied earlier, it doesn't matter how well you can clean a house because chances are, you won't be able to do it as well as professional Airbnb cleaners. If you aren't convinced yet, think about all the cleaning tricks and tips you know- how many are there?

What if you are not available to clean up the unit at a time when you have guests waiting to check-in? Will you disappoint your guests and possibly get negative feedback because of your unavailability and probably your inability to get someone else to clean the place as and when needed? You don't want that to be your property.

When you outsource cleaning services, you can be guaranteed of a spotless unit (24/7), which will impress guests, leading to greater reviews and more repeated bookings. You'd be surprised by how high people place cleanliness in a property they're paying for.

It lets you pay attention to other property management aspects

This doesn't need an explanation. You will have many things to consider when you rent out your properties, and outsourcing the cleaning responsibility enables you to focus on these other aspects fully.

It gives you more free time

It doesn't matter whether being an Airbnb is a full-time job or a side project; by outsourcing this responsibility, you can reduce the time you need to be in physical contact with the business, affording you more free time. Investing in Airbnb should be an enjoyable experience anyway. What's more, you don't need to worry about stocking up on the cleaning equipment and products.

Considering the payoffs, paying someone to manage the cleanliness of your properties is a small price to pay.

There are so many companies offering this service, but you can contact Hostmaker and let them take care of everything from beginning to end.

Other tasks you can outsource

Copywriting

Yes, a copywriter is different from a social media manager.

We noted that great listings need to have strong titles and great overall content to stand out in a crowded property market. For many people, it can be a challenge to get that text spot on every time – including those to whom creative writing comes naturally. It's not easy to write a creative listing that appeals to everyone it's meant for and drive these potential guests to book.

Note that bland headlines and ordinary or boring copy are one of the most commonly raised reasons for turning guests away from listings. It's so bad that guests don't even get to read the reviews and view all the photos; therefore, you should always ensure you attract everyone visiting your post with great words to go together with your awesome pictures. Take a look at these two posts:

Viewed 34 times in the last 48 hours

Check the calendar and pick your dates - We are filling fast.
1.6 mi to Panama City Beach center
2 BR Condo   2 BA   1100 sq ft   Sleeps 6

Viewed 54 times in the last 48 hours

A Tropical Love Nest Right on the Beach. Cruise, Beach Chairs and Drinks are on Us!
0.4 mi to Panama City Beach center
1 BR Condo   1 BA   Sleeps 6

You can see the difference, and that's reflected in the number of views.

If you are not creative enough to portray your place with the excitement and spice it deserves in the listing text; you should seriously consider outsourcing for professional help. The good thing is that we have exceptional vacation rental copywriters who can take on this task and deliver a great listing that is sure to pull readers into fantasizing about their vacation, and on toward tapping the book button. Copywriting experts such as

How to Make Your First Million Dollars With Airbnb

Guest Hook and Erin Raub are great examples who can assist you with this job.

Photography

We talked about photography at length, so you know the importance of quality photography in marketing Airbnb properties. What you need to consider as well is the fact that stunning pictures can justify higher prices as well, especially in areas where competition is not a major factor.

More managers use professional photographers to assist them to deliver these results. Even if you have time now to learn how to take pictures and how to edit them using software like Lightroom, you may not have time to practice your skills soon because the whole process takes time, especially when you're handling many properties. You need to think about getting a pro. If you're getting worried about the costs of outsourcing, let me assure you that the cost of a standard photoshoot can be recovered in your first booking.

If your properties are located in the U.S, I can recommend an expert photographer called Tyann Marcink, who is also a vacation property owner, but you can search for one in your location.

Administration and management

A huge part of the Airbnb business is fun. From creating websites, basic marketing to communicating with guests and clients, the whole business model can excite you and make you feel fulfilled. However, you can feel overwhelmed by the administration part, and it's okay to outsource for that, especially if you want to run your business partially or completely passively.

How to Make Your First Million Dollars With Airbnb

The good thing with Airbnb is that it is designed to assist you with external requirements, which include filing lodging taxes. For instance, the nature of regulations, legislation, and the imposition of lodging taxes keeps changing, and the task of filing taxes, which often gets complicated as a result, can be taken care of for you for a very modest fee. A company like [Avalara MyLodgeTax](#) can help you in researching the taxes you need to collect and remit them for you to free more of your time. This is just one example of the administrative tasks that you could be assisted with by someone who specializes in that field.

On the other hand, you can decide to sit back and collect the proceeds of your units and delegate the management tasks to someone else. The specific things the person you hire will look after will depend on your contract with them. Nonetheless, it can include things like scheduling cleanings and respond to inquiries.

As you know, outsourcing different services does cost money, and determining the ones that are best for you may also depend on your budget. What you mainly need to consider is the value of your energy and time versus the cost of getting a professional. In any case, you want your hosting experience to be hassle-free and profitable.

****

This is where I say, "that's all the investing strategies you need to know for now," we say a few words and conclude ... but you've come this far! That means you deserve something

How to Make Your First Million Dollars With Airbnb

extra- consider it a special takeaway, or a one-for-the-road of sorts —to keep you motivated.

Bonus Strategy: Try Before Buying

This is a relatively new Airbnb investing strategy that I'd want you to think about as you start your journey. Most people don't know about it.

This idea was first created by a short-term investor known as Zeona McIntyre. Some time back, a former head of hospitality at Airbnb, known as Chip Conley, mentioned that Airbnb was going into a partnership with Realtor.com. In this partnership, potential home buyers would benefit from using Airbnb to have a feel for a certain area before deciding where they want to settle. This partnership was indeed lost, but what's clear is the fact that it was designed to assist customers from both sides to broaden their customer bases.

With this strategy, that conception can be taken further.

Imagine a scenario where motivated sellers would not only list their homes with Realtor.com (or similar platforms) but also be able to list them on Airbnb to afford potential buyers a chance to try them out.

Let's take an example:

You live on a small man-made lake in Southwest Houston. Across the lake are two breathtaking lakefront homes that have been on the market for more than one year. Your one-year-long lease is about to expire, and those two townhomes were still on the market. You start to wonder why those properties are not being rented out on Airbnb to attract a broader audience of prospective buyers since they're well-staged and beautiful.

How to Make Your First Million Dollars With Airbnb

As an avid investor that you are, you wonder how frustrated the seller might be given that the homes have been on the market for far too long —even though the seller invested a good amount of money in staging them. "But I can approach the realtors or sellers and offer them a deal- to furnish and list their properties to give potential buyers a chance to try them out first- and then decide if they want to purchase them or not," you think. Indeed, this would work to assist the sellers, the frustrated realtors, and potential buyers who are "not sure."

You communicate with the parties responsible and list the properties, some potential buyers book, they like their experience there, and buy the property after the agreed period.

Win-win-win!

If that's not convincing enough, take a look at these reasons why this add-on service would work:

There's some interim revenue while showing and flexibility.

Airbnb settings are very flexible. That means that you can assist sellers in aligning their properties with their urgent need to schedule open houses and showings. This also provides a stream of revenue for sellers until the property is finally sold.

The potential buyers get to stay in the house

This is unique. Imagine being allowed to stay in a house for a couple of nights to get a feel of how it would be to stay in it during different times of day before buying it! Most buyers always have to grapple with the worry of making a wrong purchase; getting this worry out of the way puts the seller miles ahead. Any buyer would jump on this opportunity that enables them to make the best decisions for an investment as big as a home.

It's a furnished house!

Airbnb homes are typically well furnished, and such kind of homes would sell quicker for more cash. You'd be surprised by the number of people who click through images of listings on Airbnb, envisioning themselves owning the homes just by how great they look. Imagine allowing them to own the homes- beautiful and as complete as they look! What's more, the seller you'll be assisting will be able to recoup some of the costs associated with the staging or furnishing by allowing their properties to be listed on Airbnb.

It enables quick identification of maintenance issues

Since the appliances and fixtures get to be used regularly, issues will be addressed quickly- and the seller will appreciate this benefit. A house sitting for months on the market could have unseen issues like a roof leak or a hidden pipe burst, which could add to his woes.

It offers a competitive edge

This kind of add-on service is a new kid on the block, and it differentiates properties from the countless others that don't offer this service.

How to Make Your First Million Dollars With Airbnb

All these are just a few of the many reasons you should try implementing this concept, but you might wonder, "How would it work?"

The first thing you have to do is get the idea out there about the add on service: "try before buying," making sure to start by targeting your own social network. Also, target sellers, realtors and the furniture stagers who are in slow-moving markets with properties that have been sitting for between one and four months. Online services like Redfin.com can assist you with this.

When you find motivated sellers or realtors with a nice piece of property, list it on Airbnb if it has already been staged or furnish the home if it requires minor improvements so that the potential buyer gets the best experience.

Don't market the property ordinarily; market it as a "try before buying" property in the description on Realtor.com as well as on the real estate yard sign.

This concept involves collaborating with realtors, sellers, and buyers for a win-win-win; you should thus test it when you've fully established your own Airbnb business to increase your vantage point.

As we get into the last parts of the book, there are a few important things you need to note.

Tackling 2 Of The Most Common Issues In Airbnb Investing

Buying Or Investing In Property Close To You

While purchasing a house to invest in within your neighborhood comes naturally for most people, most experienced Airbnb investors strongly believe that you shouldn't necessarily buy a house just because you live there, but by making objective gauges of all the places you can invest in.

For instance, my city is great for short-term rentals, but after doing some research and math, I realized that the same house in some places was up to five times more profitable. Unfortunately, some people know this but still end up investing within their neighborhoods.

But why is this so?

For most people I've talked to about this, the one answer I always get is that "if something went wrong, I would be in a better position to fix the problem and in the process, save some money."

This means that these people end up getting less profit and doing more manual work (fixing stuff and all) – what's worse is that they don't mind it at all. It's rather odd, but it happens.

However, if you want to make good money, you have to be ready to take high risks and be smart about the numbers. For instance, if I decided to go with the property in my

How to Make Your First Million Dollars With Airbnb

neighborhood (that I found to be worth five times more in other places), I would be earning x (the possible net profit) and probably be doing manual work there. However, I decided it's better to have 5x of the profit and pay someone else to do it. I ended up having more money than I would have had and did less work. *As one expert notes, the clouding sense of comfort, security, and ignorance make some investors work more and make less money!*

One of my friends purchased her first STR property in a different state. Her first month's revenue was $10,000. In the city where she lives, the same property would have cost her twice as much, and the profit would have been half. Now she has extra revenue to pay the people working for her to do 100% of the work in that property. She must have found the strategy involving zero work more profitable because she had bought a second house in the same place (which is states away from her secure home) a few months after her first purchase.

If you invest with that in mind and manage to minimize repairs by purchasing properties in good condition, you will earn even more. This is the philosophy most successful Airbnb investors have been living by.

Some experts have also noted that labor in the cheaper markets also tends to be cheaper as well. So don't be afraid to venture into places that you cannot pass by every time you go for a morning run. You'll save yourself a ton of money, time, and energy in the long term.

In any case, I believe that your goal is to automate your business, and you can imagine how hard it can be to pay other people while experiencing tight margins!

As you do your market research, consider cities considered "most profitable."

Particularly if you don't have an idea of where to start, or are having trouble deciding between two or more cities, here're some of the places experts recommend:

Nashville, TN- Apart from enjoying a relatively lower cost of living, its biggest strength is the tourists, thanks to country music, perhaps.

Las Vegas, NV- This one requires no introduction. I can, however, mention that its high earning potential makes the lodging tax a very small price to pay for the high earnings you'll get.

Austin, TX- Airbnb is so popular here that hotel revenues have been reported to drop significantly as a result. This place hardly experiences a shortage of guests.

Chicago, IL – This place is one that overflows with events, one of them being the Lollapalooza. You can only imagine how desperate tourists would need someone like you adding more property!

Auckland, New Zealand- This is one of the most popular hosting destinations in the world, and one of the most lucrative. Also, the fact that almost everyone in New Zealand speaks English makes it even better.

Canggu, Bali- Here's a place where you can find cheap apartments that would minimize your risk, yet assuring you of high earnings. People here are friendly to foreigners, which is good for business (think tourists and yourself).

Porto, Portugal- The cost of living here is also low, and Airbnb properties here generally get rented for at least seven months in a year.

Seoul, South Korea- With prices here starting to look a bit more like they do in the US, this is a place where you'd earn a lot of cash per month by investing very little as a host.

The Potential Damages, Concerns, And Insurance

Let's start with the most commonly raised issue: partiers. Partiers have been a cause for concern for many new hosts and managers, but this is a very rare issue- and most hosts who have been in the short-term rental business long enough can agree with me.

We've had to remove vomit in the bathroom and spurts of beer in the living room, but very few times overall. As you start- before outsourcing, you can pay your cleaners double to clean such messes, and you don't even have to charge your guests more in those cases — most people who do so tend to get "revenge reviews" from unhappy guests. You also have the option of setting your cleaning fee a bit higher than the amount you pay your cleaner to account for such occasional fluctuations.

Nonetheless, you may want to note that Airbnb doesn't pay for troubles like vomit; but if such trouble made you hire someone, and have a receipt associated with the behavior, Airbnb could make them pay for it or cover it. This brings me to the second issue:

Damage to part of the property/keeping receipts

Let's say one of your guests throws a party and breaks few things or trashes the place (or both); when you report the matter to Airbnb, you'll be asked for receipts (the assumption is that if the damage was significant, you must have hired someone to fix it, and paid them). Most hosts only produce photographs, which don't help at all.

But like I said, these issues are very rare, and you're likely never going to experience them in most of your properties.

Insurance

So far, you know how Airbnb can generate cash for you and how to maximize your profit. However, you need to ensure your investment is well covered and protected in case of an emergency or to be able to fully rest assured that everything is fine.

Airbnb can be a win-win for hosts and guests alike, and having paying guests in your property always calls for a new look at the security, safety, and security measures.

Here's what you should know about protecting and insuring your listings.

Protection of your property in case of injury/damage

Generally, there are two scenarios when it comes to vacation rental insurance. If you're using the property for short-term rentals i.e. for 30 days or less, your insurance company should give you a special endorsement.

For the most part, you may have to obtain a separate insurance policy for a separate business (short-term vacation rentals) that *occurs more frequently*- this is similar to a bed and breakfast or hotel policy. Typically, a home-owners insurance policy doesn't cover for business activities.

What are the factors affecting the cost?

An insurance provider will typically charge more for a vacation rental property than a primary residence simply because they know it will stay vacant for some time, and that's a risk to them. Some of the factors affecting the cost of vacation rental insurance include the following:

- The size of your deductible- the higher it is, the lower the policy cost
- The property's location
- The value of the replacement cost- the higher the property value, the more expensive the policy is
- Rental frequency- if your property is being used as a vacation home or second home, the cost will be lower than if you used it as a typical short-term rental

- Amenities- the more the amenities, the higher the policy cost
- The average rental term- short-term rentals generally have a higher policy cost compared to long-term rentals

If you know your property will be vacant for more than 30 days, you may need to add what is referred to as a vacant property endorsement to the property so that it stays covered.

The components of short-term rental insurance

As a host, there are three main aspects you will need to think about when it comes to Airbnb insurance.

They include the following:

- Liability: this kind of insurance will protect you from the largest risk that you are exposed to as you rent your property out- YOUR GUEST. As you may already know, the risks of different liabilities that are imposed by lawsuits and property damages can be covered -of course, depending on your insurance policy. In most cases, liability insurance usually covers you during instances when you're found responsible for an accident that led to the damage of another property.
- Building and contents: the second largest risk you'll have is your actual property. In the instance your guests set a fire and burned the property down, this insurance policy aspect makes sure that your home and

all its contents are replaced based on the value you agreed upon with your insurance agent.

- The building's income: the business income is another exposure you'll have as a vacation rental owner. Your property is basically a business like any other that generates income. It's therefore prudent in some cases to protect the income of your business.

The options you have

Policies generally differ across different companies, and there are rental exposure exclusions that apply; it's, therefore, important to walk through all the worst-case scenarios. Some of the most common short-term rental insurance firms include the following:

- Proper Insurance
- HelpSafeStay
- **CBIZ**

How then do you follow-through on your policy?

Gather all the relevant information. As you obtain vacation rental insurance, it's important to gather all the information you need. If your properties offer extra recreational items like quads, bicycles, swimming pool, bikes and so forth, you have to check whether your liability insurance can cover them. Moreover, you should try to find out what support you'll have if anything went wrong and require a claim.

Who are you dealing with? Are you dealing with an agent or broker who sold you the policy or an outside source? It's important to establish a direct communication source to ease the processing of claims.

When you successfully gather all the information regarding your property, you'll have made an important step towards ensuring that your investment is well secured and insured and afforded yourself the chance to reconsider offering certain items that could expose you to personal risk.

Secondly, you need to select your policy. Armed with all the info you need, the next thing you have to do is select a policy that suits you. Each policy is categorized according to the extent of coverage, so it's important to call and discuss through your options with different representatives to make sure you're receiving the most appropriate policy for your investment. You need to be careful not to choose your insurance solely based on price. Going for the lowest priced policy may insure your vacation rental inadequately and put you in a vulnerable situation should something wrong occur.

Lastly, finalize the paperwork. You won't be protected until you finalize all the required insurance paperwork. Make sure you get all the copies of your policy before you hand the keys over to guests since you'll want to have this information on file in case of anything.

Bonus: your Airbnb insurance coverage as the Host

I hinted on this earlier, so here's the info to make it clear. Airbnb knows very well that anything can happen and therefore offers investors like you an initial insurance policy. This insurance is known as "Airbnb's Host Protection Insurance." It covers the following:

The Host Protection Insurance program: This one offers primary liability coverage that goes up to $ 1,000,000 per occurrence- that is, in the event of property damage or third-party claims of physical injury.

This program covers certain property damages in what is referred to as common property areas outside of the property itself- for instance, a building lobby. Homeowner or landlord associations are also covered in some cases in the instance claims are filed against them as a result of injury experienced by a guest or when a guest damages a building property. Certain conditions, exclusions, and limitations may apply. You also need to note that this doesn't cover everything as it is not comprehensive.

For your Airbnb investment to be fully protected, you may need business liability insurance. In case your renters damage your property, it's very unlikely that a standard homeowner's policy will reimburse the property's value. When a renter breaks or steals contents of your property, your policy may not expressly consider this a 'covered peril,' which highlights my advice that you need to double-check your level of coverage.

As most experienced hosts and property managers will tell you, protecting your investment through insurance is not the sexiest part of Airbnb investing, but it is integral to the business.

Conclusion

So, what is the ultimate way of making your first million with Airbnb?

I've outlined four strategies in the book, which are as follows:

- Buying a property and listing it, and earning off it as typical host
- Rental arbitrage- partnering with a landlord/landlady and listing their property/properties
- Managing other people's Airbnb properties
- The "stay before buying" strategy: Renting out properties being staged for sale by realtors

To make the most of this book, you can invest in the strategies in order of their appearance on my list. If it all goes well, you can be more than a millionaire within a very short period.

However, you are free to be creative and flexible.

You can decide to go with the first three methods and follow all the steps outlined in the book keenly; you'd make more than one million within 18 months. But remember that many people have netted millions using the first strategy alone, others the second alone, while others, a combination of two or more of the above methods.

It all boils down to you- your current situation (assets/financial, country, etc.), ability, and creativity. If you can buy a property, list it and buy a couple more and make your million out of it, that would be great.

If you want to start a bit more modestly and rent out part of your home and couple that with rental arbitrage, and perhaps venture into small-scale property management, you could make more than one million within a few years. All you need to do is choose your strategy carefully, and follow the steps outlined in the book from the regulations and formalizations, pricing, marketing, automation, insurance, and so forth prudently.

Above all, remember that we're talking real estate, where patience is key.

www.ingramcontent.com/pod-product-compliance
Lightning Source LLC
Chambersburg PA
CBHW070648220526
45466CB00001B/350